THE STORY OF
PICKFORDS

ARTHUR INGRAM

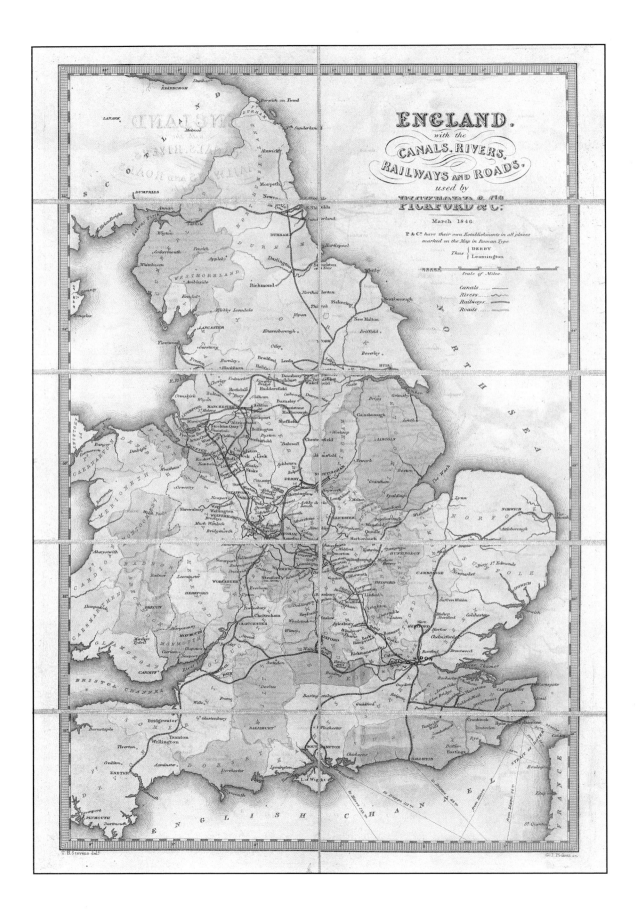

ENGLAND.
with the
CANALS, RIVERS,
RAILWAYS AND ROADS,
used by
PICKFORD & Co.
March 1846.

P & Co. have their own Establishments in all places
marked on the Map in Roman Type

Thus | DERBY
      | Leamington

Scale of Miles.

Canals ......
Rivers ......
Railways ......
Roads ......

T.H. Stevens delt.

G.J. Pickett sc.

THE STORY OF PICKFORDS

ARTHUR INGRAM

PICKFORDS
The Careful Movers

First published in 1993 by **Roundoak Publishing**
Nynehead, Wellington, Somerset, England, TA21 0BX.

©Copyright 1993 **Arthur Ingram & Roundoak Publishing**

ISBN 1 871565 16 2 Hardback
ISBN 1 871565 17 0 Softbound

Design and typesetting by **Haight Ashbury Design,
Stoke Sub Hamdon, Somerset**

Printed in Great Britain by **Spencers, Lynx Trading Estate,
Yeovil, Somerset**

Below: The Pickfords depot in Leamington
Spa was located at The Priory, an apt name
for such a genteel town! This period
photograph provides a view of the fleet,
probably typical of many of the branches,
which were in use during the 1920s. After the
steam wagons in the fleet, the Leyland 4-
tonner was next in the general progression of
things, these being supplied with platform
bodies for use with the almost universal lift
vans. Next is a pair-horse wagon complete
with lift van, whilst at the rear is the older
type of pair horse van with the driver sitting
on the roof.

Index

Author's Preface

A book of this type can rarely be described as 'all my own work', and it is equally true about this volume. Many of the photographs have come from vehicle manufacturers as well as Pickfords themselves, plus some from my own collection, but in addition I am indebted to John Aldridge, Peter Davies, Geoff Lumb and Jack London for particular items used herein. A special thanks is due to Keith Mossman for the loan of his Pickfords collection, just when I needed it.

Much of the information regarding the fleet details come from records kept by that expert of BRS, Mike Houle; plus some additional material from Gordon Mustoe, and my thanks are duly recorded.

A great deal of research time has been saved by drawing upon the book 'Traffic and Transport' by Gerard L. Turnbull, and this volume is highly recommended, for it contains a wealth of detail on Pickfords place in the transport scene of the past.

I am also indebted to the most helpful staff of Quadrant Picture Library with regard to the old files of 'Commercial Motor' and 'Motor Transport', those invaluable twins of the commercial vehicle world over the past 90 years or so: long may they flourish.

Finally, I would like to record the continual help and friendship accorded me by the staff of Pickfords, in particular Linda Schofield and Donna Armstrong — thank you ladies!

It will be noticed that the contents place greater emphasis upon the first sixty years or so of this century, rather than the period which follows. To vehicle enthusiasts, this is probably the most interesting, but with the passage of time we could perhaps see a further volume which goes into greater detail with more recent events.

This book has been produced as a follow-up to the original Pickfords volume in the 'Trucks in Britain' series which is now out of print. Those who have that book will no doubt recognise that some of the photographs have been repeated, but this is because they were of such good quality and replacements have not been found. It is hoped that this does not detract from the presentation.

Arthur Ingram
Enfield
June 1993

Some Notes on Vehicle Numbering

It has been said that Pickfords have always numbered everything, and this is confirmed by reference to old records which list horses and horse vehicles.

The advent of the self-propelled vehicle prompted a new series of numbers, with a Wallis & Steevens 3-ton tractor, A3414 being allocated fleet No.1 in 1903.

The system continued, and when Hay's Wharf Cartage took control in 1920, it was their fleet which was added into the Pickford series, not the other way round as one might expect!

A glance through old fleet lists reveals just how varied the vehicle types could be, for a batch of orders could include chassis which were destined to carry a variety of bodywork.

One chassis might be destined for Removals, while the next number was allocated to Meat Cartage. A couple of vans for a contract hire customer could be followed by a car for a representative, a service van for the Engineers, a Heavy Haulage tractor and a tilt van for the Multiple Shop department.

Similarly, the close relationship which existed with Carter, Paterson & Co. at varying levels over the years shows in the fleet list, with certain vehicles being detailed as 'CP'. The 1933 takeover of both fleets by the railways meant even closer relationship, but the two maintained their independence to a large extent, and two separate series of numbers were allocated to the two fleets.

This did give rise to certain problems, especially with spare vehicles or contract motors being in plain colour livery. Things really came to a head in 1946 with the setting up of the Carter, Paterson & Pickfords Joint Parcels Service, for here vehicles of both companies were working side-by-side.

The fact that both fleets were of similar size, and both were using plain fleet numbers of four digits, (Pickfords were up to about 4400 and CP around 3400), all contributed to confusion. Hence the CP fleet had a prefix of 1 or 10,000 added, so that it was easy to distinguish one from the other.

The original Pickfords series continued until 1957 when, as the numbers approached the magical 9999, it was decided to renumber what remained in a new series, starting at M1 for the majority of the fleet, excepting the Meat Cartage fleet which was allocated a separate series beginning X1.

This series of numbers was again succeeded by a third in 1978, starting at M1000, and to date this series has reached 5000.

Introduction

The name of Pickfords has been synonymous with transport for a very, very long time. So long in fact that its origins are shrouded in the mists of time. Some think that James Pickford was the founder of the business somewhere in the early part of the 18th century, while others believe that a certain Will Pickford was the original carrier, and he was in business around a century earlier.

Whatever the date of origin, Pickfords can be justly proud to claim that in the face of many changes to its owners and control through the ages, it still trades under the name of its founder: there are few companies with such historic roots.

The mode of actual movement has also gone through changes brought about by modern developments, with carriage being arranged by packhorse, wagons and coaches, canal boats, railways, traction engines, lorries, motor coaches and modern trucks.

Throughout its long history, one ingredient has remained: customer service. For no serious business can become established, expand and prosper without total dedication to this precept. Pickfords has succeeded by taking good care of its customers and moreover their goods, whether it has been an expensive piece of industrial equipment, or the contents of a humble home.

About 40 years separates these two photographs of Pickfords removals vehicles posed beneath the dome of St. Paul's Cathedral. The photograph far left shows one of the Bedford articulated vans of the 1940s, at a time when articulated vans of this size were being used increasingly for office and larger house removal. The photograph near left shows the style of the 1990s typified by a MAN rigid van with close-coupled drawbar trailer of greater capacity than the articulated vehicle and with enhanced flexibility in operation.

Early History

"The history of British transport for the last three hundred years, is the history of Pickfords". So ran the opening line of 'Transport Saga', the official history of the company, produced in 1947.

So now that nearly another 50 years have passed, that puts the origins of the company somewhere around 1650, but with a story stretching back so far, it is nigh impossible to say exactly when the Pickford transport business really began.

Pickfords own publication quotes 1646 as the earliest date to which a reference to Thomas Pickford can be found: that he was living at Adlington, a small village lying between Poynton and Prestbury in Cheshire. There is also evidence to show that a Will Pickford was engaged as a carrier around 1630 in the same area, and one can only guess as to any connections.

Whatever the actual origins, we know that Thomas Pickford was engaged in using packhorses for carrying, and a contemporary writer described the long caravans of packhorses which travelled the area, forty or fifty at a time.

More facts are available concerning James Pickford who was born in the early years of the 18th century, although it is not clear if he was the son of Thomas or Mathew Pickford. An advertisement in the Manchester Mercury of August 1756 is given as the earliest evidence that James was in fact a carrier between Manchester and London, but this was with wagons and not packhorses. The London terminus was stated as being The Bell Inn, Wood Street.

When James Pickford died in 1768, his widow Martha and sons Mathew and Thomas took over the business. An advertisement of 1771 stated that in future the Bear Inn in Basinghall Street was to be the London terminus for their service.

Within a short while a new service was begun — the Fly Wagon. This was a lighter, faster vehicle than the broad wheeled heavy wagons of before, and although it was not as fast as the stage coaches of the day, it was sprung, travelled further each day and was therefore able to cut the travelling time from Manchester to London down to four and a half days.

Expansion of a different kind occurred in 1777 when Pickfords took over the business of William Bass, a carrier between Burton-on-Trent, Ashbourne and Derby, who had decided to concentrate his energies to brewing beer.

By 1803 the business had expanded to such an extent that the Manchester-London service was running on six days a week, with

(Right): Taken from a series of coloured postcards issued in the 1920s, this artists impression is entitled 'Pack Horses. Pickfords earliest means of transport. 1673'. The long caravan of horses is strung out across the rolling countryside, with armed outriders making sure the horses keep a steady pace, as well as generally protecting the loads and watching out for any injuries. Note that the goods are carried in wicker basket panniers with a leather pouch on the horses back; some of the horses carry bells for identification at night and as a warning of their approach.

(Right): These old paintings are unfortunately rather crude in some respects, and a certain latitude is necessary when studying the pictures with a view to obtaining accurate detail. Entitled 'Day' and dated 1810, the view is of a cobbled yard looking out through an archway onto a shopping street. The artist shows us a Pickfords wagon being loaded/unloaded with casks, while spare horses wait nearby. The ladies being helped into a road coach at right and the well-dressed children in the foreground lead one to believe that a certain artists licence has been used in this view.

PACK HORSES. *Pickfords earliest means of transport. 1673.*

From the Oil Painting "DAY" 1810

alternative services via Buxton or Leek and Macclesfield on different days. Within a few years, services were also operating from Burton to London via Derby, and another from Sheffield to London via Leicester.

A few years earlier, in 1780, Pickfords began to route some of their traffic over the new canal system which was expanding at this time. This new sphere of transport had its origins with the Duke of Bridgewater in 1759, when he instituted the first section of narrow water channels to carry his coal from Lancashire.

Pickfords had ten boats working in 1795, this growing to 28 by 1803. Trying to mirror the road-going operation, some of the boats were slow barges while others were quoted as being 'fly-boats' or faster craft for the more expensive commodities. The canal service was not entirely independent of the road wagons, most of the traffic was destined for locations not served by the canal, so goods had to be transhipped for final delivery: the two methods were complementary.

As the traffic using the canal system increased, so Pickfords found it necessary to provide their own canal-connected facilities. In addition to a quay at the Manchester end of the operation, new wharves and warehouses were provided at Paddington, Deptford, Brentford and City Road, all in the London catchment area. They also set up smaller facilities at many points along the canal routes, where goods might be delivered or transhipped.

As the years went by the family firm prospered, and after the death of Martha Pickford the sons of Thomas and Mathew started to become interested in the business. Early in the 19th century we read that the business was in the hands of 'Thomas and Mathew' and 'James and Mathew',

Entitled 'Regent's Canal — East entrance to Islington Tunnel', this view shows two of Pickfords canal boats in a lock at the London end of the canal, not far from City Basin, their main dock and warehouse.

the duplication of names causing some confusion, although Mathew II was the son of Thomas, and Mathew III son of Mathew I.

New services were established, and some of the earlier routes and journey times were improved. The canal system was expanded and Pickfords added to its fleet of canal boats to take up the expansion of business. As time moved on, so did the family, and in 1800 we read of 'Thomas and James Pickford & Company'. Shareholders in this company included Thomas, Thomas II, Mathew II and Mathew III, each having an equal majority holding, the balance being shared between four others in a larger spread of the family. Thomas II and Mathew III were in charge at Manchester, while James and Mathew II looked after the London end.

There next followed a period of some problems and a downturn in trade, for although Pickfords expansion had been exceptional: almost 20 depots and wharves in 1803 to over 50 by 1817, the company was in financial trouble and the pressures were on.

The expansion might have been too swift or trading conditions may have shrunk, whatever the explanation, the company took a major blow when James and Mathew II withdrew, and took their capital with them.

The next chapter of the story begins in 1817, for this was the year when Joseph Baxendale entered the Pickford business along with Zachary Langton and Charles Inman, all three being connected by family and having access to the level of capital necessary to rescue the company from complete obscurity.

Joseph Baxendale was the real power in the new Pickford & Company, set up on April 1st 1817. He originated from Lancaster and had been in the cotton trade, working in London. Thomas Pickford and Baxendale took control of the head office of the business at Manchester, while Mathew Pickford and Langton looked after the London end of things. Charles Inman was positioned at Leicester. Interestingly the new firm traded as T & M Pickford & Co. in Manchester, but as Mathew Pickford & Co. in London.

The energetic and forceful manner in which Baxendale set about getting the firm back on to a sound footing, is recounted in the 1947 history.

He toured the company depots and the road and canal routes they used, checking on every facet of the operation, observing the staff and making comments in no uncertain manner. He gained a first-hand knowledge of the whole extent of the business, a knowledge that was to be critical for the future of the company.

It was not to be long before a new upheaval was upon the carrying trade, for following quickly upon the establishment of the canal system was the introduction of the railway: inland transport and the carriers were in for an even greater challenge.

Baxendale viewed the newcomer similarly to that of the canals, and decided that collaboration was far better than confrontation. The Liverpool and Manchester Railway was the first to be tackled by Baxendale, and although they did not want him to handle their goods traffic as he would have liked, they did discuss special terms for the movement of Pickfords vans.

Contemporary description suggests that the van bodies were to be

(Right): This well-known painting shows the famous Pickfords Fly Wagon or high speed van, used for the prestigious fast journeys for high value goods. The very best drivers were employed on this service and an armed guard was carried to ward off any would-be highway robbers.

(Right): The last in the series of old advertising postcards, is this double view of early railway practice. Entitled 'Goods Train, London & Manchester Railway 1833', the upper train is pictured with a couple of wagons being used by Pickfords, as their tarpaulins show.

transferred from railway wagon to carts with wheels at the terminus, thus originating the idea of containers, swap bodies or lift vans. Later on Pickfords horsedrawn pantechnicons were taken by rail, and of course the railways were heavily engaged in container traffic of their own, much later.

Other railway companies were approached with the idea of them being used for at least part of the journey for goods consigned between the industrial centres, such as Liverpool, Manchester, Birmingham and London. Some progress was made, and traffic did pass over some of the expanding network, but many problems arose between established carriers such as Pickfords, and the new railway companies who visualised tremendous potential in their new-found speedy routes which paralleled the old canals.

One such problem was that of Pickfords using hampers for 'bulking' smaller parcels. This was perhaps an accepted way of handling a number of small packages, which were all consigned to a common destination, being sorted there for the individual delivery. But the railways did not see it that way. They accused Pickfords of avoiding the full payment for a number of packages, by packing them into one larger container.

But there were many independent railway companies and not all viewed the carriers with such antipathy. The London & Birmingham was more acceptable to carriers using the railway for either all or part of the journey for consignments, and Baxendale was keen to exploit such potential to the full.

He explained to the directors of the London & Birmingham that he could visualise a great increase in traffic as the railway network was expanded and connected across the country. He wanted Pickfords to have a stake in that and so set about providing a vast new depot at Camden Town primarily to take advantage of the expected increase in rail-borne traffic.

The new depot, which included warehousing, stabling and offices was built on the south side of the Regent's canal, opposite to the existing Camden depot of the railway. A bridge was built over the canal to connect the two depots, and facilities were installed for the easy transfer of goods between canal barges, the depot and the rail connection.

The new complex was opened in December 1841, but its expected success was short-lived. A long and costly legal battle between Pickfords, and other carriers, and the Grand Junction Railway in the 1840s, led to Pickfords not using that line for its traffic to and from the Manchester area. This meant having to find alternative routes which were longer and therefore slower or resorting to transhipping loads between available services, such as canal routes or even road.

The real crunch came in the middle 1840s when the Grand Junction, Liverpool & Manchester, Manchester & Birmingham and London & Birmingham railway companies agreed to amalgamate, thus forming the London & North Western Railway. Soon the new company decided to handle goods traffic themselves, at the expense of the carriers, and only Pickfords and Chaplin & Horne were granted the business of being Agents for the company.

This arrangement continued for the next twenty years or so with the

(Right): Although dated 1912, this Pickfords letter heading could well be much older. It illustrates the main areas of operation which the company wished to publicise, showing as it does Pickford's Wharf, a Pickford container being conveyed by train, an old horsedrawn pantechnicon being drawn by a steam tractor and a single horse van marked City & Suburban Hourly Express. The old Pickford flag which shows a packhorse is also displayed at top left.

(Right): Entitled 'Pickford's Steam Road Van', this view purports to show an early self-propelled steam vehicle approaching a toll gate, with the usual public house alongside. From what we can ascertain, the vehicle is a closed van with additional load carried on the roof. From the position of the chimney we must assume that it was rear-engined, particularly as the stoker is pictured with what appears to be coal in a shute at the rear. How the goods were loaded into the body is a mystery. No confirmation has been discovered that such vehicles were ever operated, and the picture may have been produced in order to fill a gap in the supposed history of Pickfords transport.

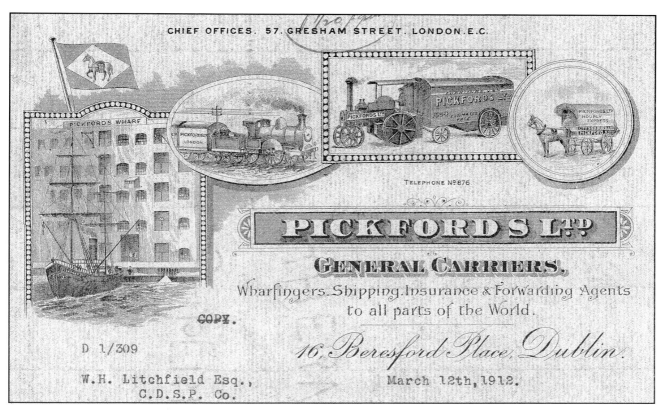

CHIEF OFFICES. 57. GRESHAM STREET. LONDON. E.C.

PICKFORDS WHARF

TELEPHONE N⁰ 876

PICKFORDS L™

GENERAL CARRIERS,

Wharfingers. Shipping. Insurance & Forwarding Agents
to all parts of the World.

COPY.

16, Beresford Place, Dublin.

D 1/309

March 12th, 1912.

W.H. Litchfield Esq.,
C.D.S.P. Co.

PICKFORD'S VAN
LONDON & MANCHESTER

THE BULL HEAD INN

Pickford's STEAM ROAD VAN.

period marked by one sort of hiccup or another. There were arguments between the two Agents as well as with the railway company itself, and by the mid 1860s the agreement was just about ready to fall apart.

The LNWR absorbed Chaplin & Horne in 1877, but Pickfords remained, although on a different basis of the agreement — it being merely of six-month tenure.

One little item that is worth recording, is that Pickfords had a driver working for them named James Paterson. His job was in the border area between England and Scotland, an area that was increasingly under threat from railway dominance. Pickfords share of traffic fell dramatically, and James Paterson found himself out of a job.

He travelled to London to see what it had to offer a young man with carrying experience. Making contact with Walter Carter who owned a carrying business in Manchester, they formed a partnership to establish a business based in London. So Carter, Paterson & Co. came on the scene, a name which was to dominate the London carrying trade through to 1949, and be in varying levels of competition and co-operation with Pickfords during the period in between.

As time progressed, the railways realised their potential for freight traffic as well as that of passengers, gradually moving to exclude the road carriers from much of the lucrative work emanating from collection and delivery services. They either set up their own C&D services or expanded those already existing, by adding yet more horses and vans.

These were the days of the great Victorian expansion, with trade and industry demanding even better quality service from the carriers, especially that of speed of delivery from the mills, factories, warehouses and stores. The railways naturally benefited from this increase in traffic, but competition was fierce and the road carriers were not slow in seizing the opportunities offered, with established firms like Pickfords and comparative newcomers in the shape of Carter, Paterson.

Many customers of the road carriers put their faith in the name on the van which came to the door, caring little, or rather being ignorant, as to which route the goods took to their destination. It was up to the established carriers such as Pickfords to maintain that bond of trust.

In the large towns and cities, road traffic was increasing with all this activity, and this meant one thing — more horses. Contemporary accounts tell of the problems brought about by the jostling horse teams, whether they be those of the carriers, traders, brewers or millers. The narrow streets became congested, carts broke down, horses collapsed, the manure piled up and the smell on a hot day...

Small boys were sometimes employed to keep the streets clear of the horse droppings, horse protection societies did their best to improve conditions for the animals, and the one saviour on the horizon was — the motor vehicle.

Top right: Always with an eye for publicity, Pickfords managed to get one of their single horse wagons photographed for the press when it was engaged in transporting a load of Shell motor spirit. The occasion was the 1910 Antarctic Expedition led by the famous Captain Scott , and the petrol was for his motor sleigh. His ship, the Terra Nova, can be seen in the background.

Bottom right: An early undated photograph showing one of the trotting vans employed for the parcel express service in the days before motor vans. Judging by the amount of flowers and ribbons decorating the harness, the single horse van is prepared for entry into a local carnival or the decoration might be in celebration of a royal occasion. The local address of Blackstock Road, Finsbury Park was later to be the location of the headquarters of the Household Removals department.

Above: Indicative of Pickfords attitude to publicity is the fact that they were constantly issuing notices, handbills, trade cards and booklets advertising the very many facets of the business, right through from the early days of pack-horses, fly wagons, canals and railways, continuing into modern times. Copies of early notices survive which list the many towns to which they would carry your goods and valuables, with lithographs being used to show the mode of transport being used. With the advent of photography it was possible to show actual vehicles, and the scenery van depicted here comes from a little 50-page publication of 1910 entitled Pickfords' Pocket Guide which includes copious information on their services as well as useful lists of postal and telegraph rates, and a list of times for post to foreign parts.

The Motor Age Begins

With a company such as Pickfords, which was established so long ago, the actual date when mechanical transport was first used, is difficult to verify.

From the motor vehicle fleet list, No.1 was a 1903 Wallis & Steevens 3-ton steam tractor, but it is possible that any experimental vehicles acquired prior to this date, might well have been numbered in the old numbering system which was used for the horsedrawn vehicles.

Reference to the fleet list shows that the first batches of steam vehicles were numbered consecutively in date order as acquired, although not all were bought new. Photographs of the earliest vehicles show that they were in fact numbered, confirming information from other sources.

So the earliest vehicles were Wallis & Steevens steam tractors used to tow the old horsedrawn pantechnicons and trailers for removals or haulage work. One report mentions that in September 1903 there were just two in service, while another says that by November there were 20 in use.

An experimental James & Browne petrol van was acquired in 1904 in order to service a contract with St. Bartholemews Hospital, which entailed transport from the laundry at Swanley. The daily journeys were reported to have been seriously interrupted by frequent breakdowns, so the van was withdrawn and the service reverted to a trotting van.

In 1904 the steam vehicles were used for the bulk transfer of loads between the warehouse at City Basin off City Road, and the depots at Brentford, Fulham and Kingston. A solitary English steam van was tried out in 1905, followed by the Hindley, which is the type reputed to really have put Pickfords steam haulage onto a firm foundation.

A batch of Hindleys followed in 1906, and with them came the engineer William Elliott, supplied to maintain the wagons and to train the staff. He stayed with Pickfords, and more will be heard of him later. This year marked the start of steam vans being used for meat deliveries from Smithfield market to retail shops.

In the same year a report said that a James & Browne 2-ton van (!), was being used for deliveries of the Daily Mail and the Daily Mirror to several

Above: This rather old and battered picture from an unknown source, is interesting in that it shows one of the depots with a mixture of both horse and steam traction. Nearest is a pair horse van, whilst next to that is a similar van but with a steam tractor attached. This is carried on what appears to be solid wheels with separate block treads, while the rear wheels have tangential spokes. A larger steam tractor is standing against the building at the rear, while what appears to be a steam wagon is just visible at the far end of the canopy.

Right: The change over from horse to steam traction is abundantly clear in this view of one of the early Wallis & Steevens road tractors, which is coupled to a rather battered pantechnicon. The van is of the 'Purdy' type with the integral well and recessed large diameter wheels, while the small front wheels enable a tight turning circle to be accomplished as they can pass under the floor without fouling. The bags on the roof probably contain extra fuel for the tractor and they are secured by the ten-inch high roof boards. In good removals practice the substantial tailboard is regularly used.

Top right: This somewhat poor quality photograph shows an early design of steam wagon marketed by the English Steam Wagon Co. of Hebden Bridge for about three years in the early part of this century. It was of American design and had a vertical boiler mounted on the front platform which supplied power to a horizontal engine lying amidships with gear drive to the rear wheels. The vehicle carries the number 26 in the Pickfords fleet, but how many were used is not known. The feature of large diameter rear wheels is not unusual for the period, and the general design owes much to contemporary horsedrawn vehicles.

Middle right: This rather dark and yellowy period photograph shows one of the small Wallis & Steevens steam tractors all steamed up and ready to go after loading the statue 'Physical Excellence' for its journey to Southern Rhodesia where it was to be erected in honour of Cecil Rhodes. A wooden trestle is provided to support the belly of the horse as it is carried on the solid trailer over the unforgiving roads of the day. The tractor appears to be one of the first batch to be acquired by the company toward the end of 1903 soon after the passing of the first motor registration regulations enacted by The Motor Car Act of 1903 and the Motor Car (Registration and Licensing) Order of the same year.

south coast resorts. One can only guess whether this was the Barts laundry van being given a second chance.

No matter how good the Hindley wagons were reputed to be, they were not continued with, and Aveling & Porter and Wallis & Steevens wagons and tractors, helped swell the fleet in the next few years. A Burrell tractor joined the fleet and a large batch of Foden wagons were bought, some of them secondhand.

A contemporary photograph of one of Pickfords vehicles shows it displaying a poster announcing that they had '83 motors at work in London', a total not borne out by subsequent fleet records, so perhaps it included hired vehicles.

In September 1907 a Foster 'Wellington' tractor was exhibited at the Smithfield Show, it being advertised as the "third of its type for Pickfords". Unusually it was mounted on special Tangent wheels where the spokes are arranged tangentially and not radially as standard.

Competition in the parcels carrying business was increasing with MacNamara, Beans Express, Suttons and Globe Express, in addition to that of Carter, Paterson & Co. who had just established two subsidiaries — London & Provincial Motor Despatch Co. and The London Motor Parcels Express Ltd. Pickfords responded with the Motor Cartage & Carrying Co. and in 1908 they acquired a small undertaking, The Motor Delivery Co.

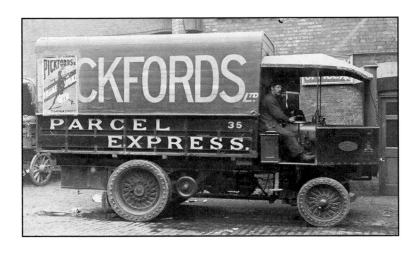

Above: Photographs of the early Hindley steam wagons supplied to Pickfords show them mounted on the then current style of heavy steel spoked wheels, but after a while the tangential-spoked wheels as displayed on Wagon No. 35 were preferred. Note the poster advertising 'Luggage in Advance' which has been added rather haphazardly to the boarded tilt cover in this 1905 photograph.

By 1908 depots had been established at:

Balham	Deptford	Penge
Berwick Street	Edmonton	Poplar
Bishopsgate	Finsbury Park	Pimlico & Brompton
Brentford	Fulham	Stratford
Bricklayer's Arms	Gt. Tower Street	Walthamstow
Brixton	Kingston	Wharf, Clink Street
Broad Street	Lee	Whitechapel
City Basin	Long Lane	Willow Walk
Chalk Farm	Marylebone	Woolwich
Croydon	Paddington	York Road

In addition the company had no less than 62 provincial addresses which it called 'Country Agencies', these varying from full size depots down to booking and receiving offices.

The importance of the new steam and petrol motors to the operation of the company's services, is reflected by the fact that new premises were acquired at Hackford Road, Brixton in 1910, purely for the upkeep and repair of them.

Although Pickfords were busy buying additional steam wagons right up to, and after the Great War, its rival, Carter, Paterson & Co. disposed of their

Right: A copy from an old trade card issued by the Eastbourne branch shows a contemporary view of a typical removals outfit of the period. The Aveling & Porter overtype wagon displays how almost half its length is taken up by the boiler, engine and crew, leaving the high flat body barely large enough to accommodate the lift van. As to be expected, the pantechnicon trailer with a well floor and cranked rear axle, is of horsedrawn parentage, and the drivers high-perched seat remains for use by one of the crew for braking the trailer.

Top right: Recorded as Fleet No.102, this Wallis & Steevens wagon was built toward the end of 1911, and is reported as entering service early in the following year. Pickfords bought around a dozen Wallis & Steevens wagons of both 3- and 5-ton types during the period 1906-1912. With a variety of body styles, including flat, sided and tilt van, they were mounted on either steel or wooden wheels, and the majority came on rubber tyres.

Middle right: Pickfords must have been instrumental in giving the little firm of E.S. Hindley & Sons a tremendous boost to their business of steam wagon building in the early part of the century. The design of vehicle was adequately reported upon in the trade press of the day, and the company took steps to advertise the fact that they had been blessed with repeat orders. All this even in the face of competition from other better-known wagon builders such as Aveling & Porter, Foden and Wallis & Steevens from whom Pickfords had obtained wagons. The wagon depicted in this advertisement shows the original type which was supplied with the old steel wheels; later additions to the fleet were specified with wooden wheels with tangentially-arranged spokes, to the Gare pattern.

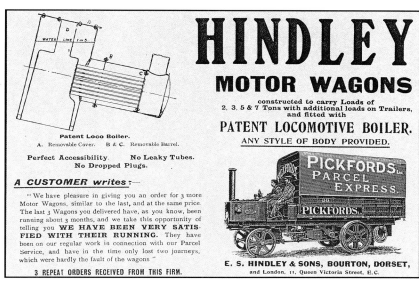

last steam vehicle in 1911. This might sound startling, but it should be remembered that much of Pickfords work was haulage of all kinds, whereas CP & Co's was parcels.

By 1912 the first petrol motors were being tried out, with Berna, Commer, Thornycroft and Tilling types among them. The year was important because it saw a degree of co-operation come into the highly competitive parcels business in London. Agreement was reached between the main contenders with the result that CP & Co took over the parcels work of Pickfords, in addition Beans Express and the London Parcels Delivery Co. joined in. The scheme was run by CP in London and Pickfords in the provinces, with Beans acting only as a collection agency.

The year also saw another important development — the formation of Hay's Wharf Cartage, a company of which we hear more later.

At the 7th Commercial Motor Users Association Parade of Vehicles held in London in 1913, Pickfords entered 18 vehicles, including Aveling, Commer, Thornycroft and Wallis types. Whilst at the 1914 Brussels Motor Show a new type of 2½-ton Minerva lorry was exhibited which had been sold to Pickfords. It was of forward control type with the Knight engine set between the front seats. The final drive was by overhead worm, it had cast steel wheels and a body 10ft 6in long.

In February 1913 a newcomer in the field of parcels carriers was established — W&G. This new company was created by the important motor-based du Cros organisation based at Acton in west London, and was innovative by virtue of the fact that the vehicles were all motor vans.

By 1913 they were operating a fleet of 100 vans in the London area, and it was seen as a thorn in the side of Carter, Paterson who, since their agreement with Pickfords and the other carriers, had looked upon London as their slice of the business.

As things turned out they need not have worried. 1914 came and with it the Great War. W&G turned their motor expertise to things military, the parcels business took a downturn, and the result was that W&G sold their parcels business to CP in 1915.

As the Great War ended and things returned to something like normality, Pickfords took stock of the situation and looked ahead to expansion of their motor fleet. It was still predominantly steam powered, but the war had proved the feasibility of heavier petrol driven motors and within a short while new names appeared in the fleet roster, such as Leyland and Knox.

The company still had almost 1600 horses and 1900 horse vans in service, so replacement was going to take some time...

Below: Typical of the early petrol motor lorries of the first decade of the century, is this RC model Commer with open chain drive and chassis frame strengthened by tie rods. The leather-gaitered and uniformed driver is afforded little comfort, sitting on a non-adjustable wooden bench seat with the fold-down semi-circular hood in case it rains. The controls can be clearly seen, the lever for selecting the gears being positioned on the right of the steering column just below the driver's right hand, for this is one of the Commers with the Linley pre-selector gearbox, which can be seen midway beneath the chassis frame. Interestingly no horn is fitted to this vehicle, a bell is positioned at the extreme end of the driver's seat. Note that two fleet numbers are carried — 40 on the body and 74 on the chassis, and this is probably because the body has been transferred from No.40 which was a Hindley steam wagon.

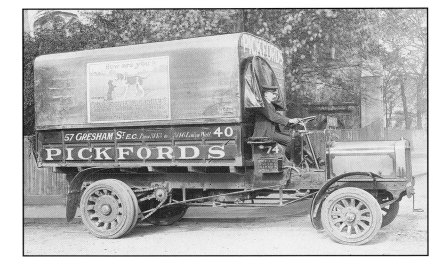

Bottom right: Haulage as it was. A pair of Foden steam wagons operating from the Eastbourne branch show the variety of traffic handled in these days of early mechanical traction. The leading wagon is well loaded with an assortment of packing cases and a sheet thrown over to keep the weather off those that it covers, while the trailer is obviously of the horsedrawn pantechnicon type with recesses in the body for the rear wheels. The driver has much faith in the roof boards of the van trailer for the load on the roof appears to be secured by just one strand of rope! The wagon and trailer following are loaded with a substantial stack of wide sawn timber.

Top right: Several makes of early petrol vehicles were tried in the first decade of the century, including a small number of Thornycrofts. These A-type 30cwt chassis have their transmission chains totally enclosed in cases which help to keep down noise, as well as lessening chain wear through road grit being absorbed into the links and onto the sprockets. It is interesting to note the van poster advertising the Contracts service of Pickfords, and to see that they marketed the old-style steam vehicles for their heavy hauling ability, while the petrol motors were more suited to the speedy delivery of lighter loads.

Middle right: Pickfords acquired Chaplin & Co. in 1936, and in doing so took over the control of a company which had a long history in the transport business, not unlike its own. They were road coach operators, railway cartage agents, removals contractors and small boat operators. Shown here is one of their fleet of Foden steam wagons with liftvan and ex-horsedrawn pantechnicon trailer.

Top left: Unfortunately this old postcard is rather dark and the Knox tractor difficult to see clearly, but it does provide an interesting illustration of the way in which 12"x12" long timber piles were carried. The front two feet of the long load is supported by the swivelling bolster on the Knox, being secured by five rounds of chain. At the rear end the load is supported by a single, unbraked solid axle, and tied on with a couple of loops of chain. A length of chain runs from the front bolster to the rear axle frame, and there is probably another length on the nearside, these presumably being to tie the two ends of the vehicle together. The outfit appears to be devoid of any lighting save for a solitary hurricane lamp at the rear end, and although the driver sits on a deep-buttoned leather seat, he is provided with an apology for a roof! Note that the Hackford Road address has been deleted in favour of Tower Bridge Road depot, so the date is probably near 1922.

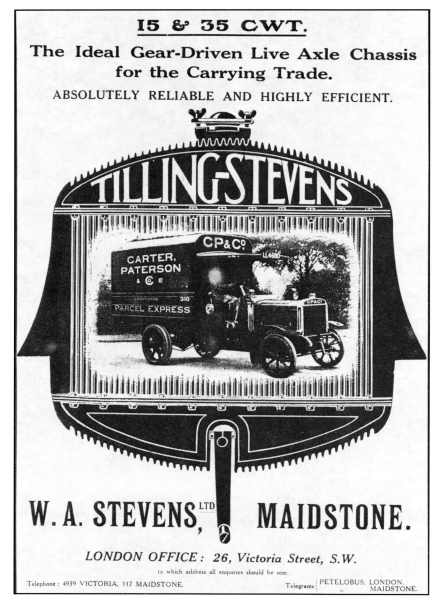

Left: This reproduction of a 1914 advertisement for Tilling-Stevens shows one of the small gear-driven chassis as opposed to the petrol-electric type for which the manufacturer was better known. Although the van is lettered in the Carter, Paterson & Co. fleet livery and even has a CP&CO insignia on the radiator header tank, closer inspection of the photograph reveals the name 'Pickfords' just above the Parcels Express legend on the bodyside. This was the period when the two great names in the London carrying business had joined forces by an amalgamation of 1912 which also included Beans Express and the London Parcels Delivery Co. and was perpetuated for the period of the Great War.

Bottom right: A scene in Fulham, south west London as the Pickfords gang prepare to move this huge rectangular tank from the two small trailers supporting it. The Foden 5-ton wagon is one of the large number acquired during the second decade of this century for a variety of haulage duties, and it is not clear from the photograph whether wagon No.179 was responsible for delivering the load or merely helping with the unloading. In the background can be seen the works of the Limmer & Trinidad Lake Asphalt Company, a firm well known for road surfacing contracts.

Right: A rather dull photograph this, but included never-the-less because it shows one of the old Leylands used on the meat delivery service being loaded at Smithfield Central Meat Markets. Hardly discernable, the side board reads 'Regular Service from Smithfield Market to Walthamstow, Chingford, Woodford, Buckhurst Hill and Loughton'. The lower part of the bodywork is well constructed with ample bracing to withstand the heavy wear encountered with the handling of heavy and rigid frozen meat carcasses such as those stacked on the barrows alongside. The load is merely covered with a tilt sheet stretched over hoops and boards to keep off the worst of the weather.

With Hay's Wharf

n 1919 new developments began, a series of discussions took place with Hay's Wharf about a possible acquisition of Pickfords; the gradual move away from using the railways began, and a completely new departure in touring coach operation took place.

The move away from use of the railways for long distance removals, was made possible by the increasing reliability of the motor fleet. The possible takeover by Hay's Wharf was an ongoing thing, so let us look in greater detail at the new coach service.

Pickfords had quite a number of Tilling-Stevens in use, they being used probably because of the ease of training staff to handle this new mode of haulage. The petrol-electric system of drive to the rear wheels did away with the need to have a change-gear mechanism, so making it easier for one to master the control of the machine.

With no gear changes taking place, the ride could be described as less stressful, and this applied to driver and any passengers alike. So it is not surprising that so many emerging bus and coach services took to the design, and Pickfords was one of them.

Below: One of the Saurer touring coaches pictured just after completion, with the usual small boy jockeying for position to be included in the photograph! These were the vehicles described as being finished in deep maroon and having very well upholstered seats so necessary for extended tours both in Britain and in continental Europe. The folding hood is stowed in a special compartment at the rear and passengers' luggage was placed in the lockers below the floor.

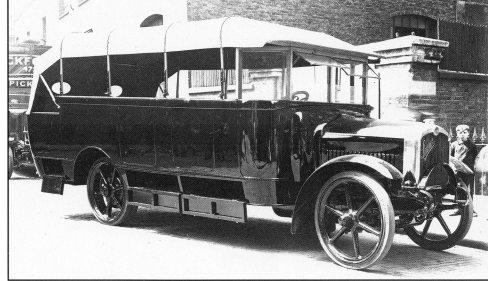

In the first year of operation four Tilling coaches were used, and whether these were originally lorries rebodied, or new chassis bought for the service is not clear. The chassis chosen was the makers 4-ton model with a 40hp engine, and for that first season seven grand tours were arranged to places in England and Wales.

So successful was the first year of operation that a further 11 new Tilling-Stevens chassis were ordered for the 1920 season. The makers 45hp and 55hp engine were specified, these being allocated according to the

Right: The Saurer Commercial Vehicle Co. was justifiably proud of the fact that Pickfords had very many of their vehicles in use in the 1920s, using them for a variety of tasks including meat, heavy haulage and removals. This reproduction of a 1925 advertisement, which graced the front cover of Motor Transport in March, 1925, not only showed one of the current fleet of Saurers but also referred to the well-publicised Pickfords Fly Wagon of some 150 years earlier.

New Passenger-carrying Vehicles. 3D

MOTOR TRANSPORT

GOODS AND PASSENGER CARRYING BY ROAD.

No. 1,044, Vol. XL. MONDAY, MARCH 2nd, 1925. THREEPENCE.
COPYRIGHT—REGISTERED AS A NEWSPAPER FOR TRANSMISSION IN THE U.K.

TRANSPORT ANCIENT AND MODERN.

1771

The highest expression of express transport in the eighteenth century was that of Messrs. Pickfords, who instituted what was then a revolution in the rapid transport of goods by means of their "FLY WAGON."

This covered the distance from London to Manchester—some 200 miles—in 5½ days, carrying about two tons, or some 72 ton miles a day.

One of Messrs. Pickfords' "Fly Wagons."

1925

Twentieth century conditions call for more rapid transport of heavy loads than was ever dreamed of by our forefathers. Messrs. Pickfords, appreciating the advantages of the most up-to-date means of transporting heavy loads, have adopted SAURER CHASSIS which, hauling trailers, will easily cover 100 miles in a day, carrying 11-ton loads, or some 1,100 ton miles a day, and can do this year after year with unfailing regularity.

THE SAURER COMMERCIAL VEHICLE Co. Ltd., 31, Augustus Street, London, N.W.1.

One of Messrs. Pickfords' Saurer Wagons with Trailer.

Saurers Save Pence per Mile

Below: Introduced in 1924 at a time when the household removals fleet was largely made up of Foden, Saurer and Leyland rigid types, this Carrimore articulated pantechnicon was something of a revelation. With a capacity of 1200cu.ft., the body was certainly an improvement on the rigid vans and lift vans in use at that time. With no drive line or axle beneath the floor, a long well added to the overall interior height, and enabled heavy goods to be loaded with ease, according to the manufacturer's brochure. The tractor part of the outfit was a standard RAF-type Leyland.

REMOVAL & STORAGE PICKFORDS HOLDENHURST RD., BOURNEMOUTH

severity of the tour. In their report on the new vehicles, the Commercial Motor mentions that special attention had been given by the chassis makers, to the brakes, "so that no fear need be felt by the nervous-inclined when descending steep hills".

Of only 23-seat capacity, the bodywork was of the open chars-a-banc type with folding canvas hood, but with just two doors on the nearside for the passengers. Seating was most comfortable, with two rows of seats separated by the central aisle, but with each seat slightly staggered from that alongside. A row of five across the back completed the layout, while a large space at the rear accommodated luggage and room for the stowed hood.

Some of the bodies were supplied by Tilling-Stevens but others were built by Birch Brothers and the Regent Carriage Co. They were finished in a rich claret colour. For some unexplained reason some of the vehicles carried IT (Leitrim CC, Ireland) registrations.

The 1920 season embraced tours varying from 7 days touring north and south Devon to one lasting 17 days which covered the Lake District and Scotland.

In 1921 the tours were extended to include Switzerland and for this the first Saurer chassis were obtained. This decision was instrumental in further orders for 50 Saurer lorries to be added to the fleet.

In addition to the regular tours advertised for each coaching season, the company also arranged special trips to events such as the Aldershot Military Tattoo, Ascot Races, as well as London sightseeing tours.

One such special event, organised by the Cardiff branch for its local customers, must rank as a bargain, even in 1927. For just £1, customers were conveyed by train to Paddington, where they were met by a Pickfords coach for a two-hour London sightseeing tour. A seat at a west end theatre followed, and then back to Paddington, where they were put back on the train for Cardiff, and treated to supper enroute!

In 1920 Pickfords was acquired by Hay's Wharf Cartage who had a considerable meat cartage business, as well as handling large quantities of provisions imported from Scandinavia and the British Dominions.

This new arrangement brought the Hay's Wharf vehicles into the Pickfords organisation, and their steam wagons and electric vans were absorbed into the system.

The first Knox tractor was acquired in 1919, and further examples were taken into the fleet, when the potential of this vehicle became apparent. Believed to be the forerunner of the Scammell which was to appear shortly afterwards, the American-built Knox had proved itself in military use during the Great War. In one report a Knox was used to transport a Winget block-making machine to Leicester, where the council were building 12,000 houses. It was said that the machine could produce sufficient blocks to build 20 houses a week.

Pickfords moved into a new area of haulage in 1921 with the takeover of B.T. Norris Ltd., a small bulk tanker business located at Gatton Motor Works, Tooting in south London. This added 14 Hallfords to the fleet.

Other makes of vehicle appeared in the fleet during this period of trial

Bottom right: The first of a pair of Pickfords coaches pulls away from the loading point in Newton Street, just around the corner from the old headquarters and removals offices in High Holborn, narrowly missing the horsedrawn van which has brought some of the passengers' luggage. All the buildings shown in this 1922 view have long since disappeared.

Right: Probably photographed just below Plymouth Hoe, this magnificent Swiss-built Saurer and trailer represented the mainstay of the long distance Removals and Storage part of the contemporary Pickfords fleet during the 1920s. This was the period when lift vans, or containers in to-day's terms, were found to be expedient and flexible in the field of removals, being able to be detached for storage or transfered to other vehicles or to railway wagons. The Saurer was a quality product, much liked by both management and drivers. This example has an ample reserve supply of petrol in the regulation two-gallon cans, rendered necessary by journeys to areas where supplies might be doubtful.

Middle right: This view of the Gales Gardens depot of City & Suburban Carriers serves to show what could be called a typical carriers yard of the 1920s. As with many other businesses, the arches of the railway passing overhead are used as the covered part of the facility, where the parcels would be unloaded, sorted and reloaded for delivery. City & Suburban Carriers were later absorbed into Carter, Paterson & Co.'s business, and the depot became part of the Carter, Paterson & Pickfords Engineers department.

for the petrol motor, with names like W&G, Daimler, Pierce Arrow, Crossley and Ford being obtained.

In 1923 the business of Robert Hall was taken over, this being a fairly large meat delivery company. The fleet was expanded by the addition of 20 4-ton Hallfords, half-a-dozen Ford model Ts and four of the unusual CPT 25cwt vans. Ten Foden steam wagons also joined the fleet at this time. Listed as coming from R. Cornell, they might well have been vehicles on contract for Robert Hall.

Interestingly, another addition to the fleet was No.515, a Diatto car, this being allocated to William Elliott, the vehicle engineer mentioned earlier. Pickfords numbered all their stock in the fleet, including cars for the staff, and the motorcycles allocated to some of the representatives.

Mention was made earlier as to the Saurers which joined the fleet from 1921 onwards. They were not obtained in very large batches, although the total reached around 100 by 1929 when the last appears to have been obtained. An indication of the importance attached to the Pickfords name appearing on the vehicles, is seen by a Saurer publication of 1926 entitled 'Transport That Saves Pence per Mile'. There are no less than three vehicles depicted in Pickfords colours, plus one in the livery of Hay's Wharf Cartage and another painted in McDougalls colours, but is actually a Pickford contract vehicle.

In 1922 the depot at Tower Bridge Road was opened, and the maintenance workshops from Hackford Road transferred there. It subsequently became one of the heavy haulage depots, but many Pickfords depots had to serve more than one section of the organisation, so in many cases a location was used as a base for several departments. Tower Bridge Road was additionally listed as a garage for Hay's Wharf Cartage vehicles.

A new departure took place in 1929 with the establishment of the Multiple Shop department. This was originally begun in order to service the shops of the Home & Colonial group which included Maypole Dairies, Liptons, Pearks and Meadow Dairies.

The mid 1920s saw the fleet expand as the business increased, although some vehicles were taken into the fleet, only to be disposed of in just a few years. Whether this was due to the types not being standard to Pickfords or whether the work on which they were employed disappeared, is not clear.

Straker-Squire, Trojan, Bean, Scammell, Morris and Chevrolet makes appear in the fleet list, some never to appear again, while others were to herald a switch to that particular make for quite large numbers. The first Ransomes & Rapier mobile crane appears in the 1925, obtained it is said after being on exhibition at the 1924 Wembley Empire Exhibition.

A few McCormick tractors are purchased, so useful for handling meat

Below: Many Morris cars and Morris-Commercial vans were used in the fleet during the 1920s and 1930s, from the little 'Minor' through to quite large six-wheelers, but the arrival of the Bedfords soon brought that to an end. This old advertising postcard shows one of the many 1-ton vans used by Household Removals, it being a 1924 model with bodywork by Wilson of Kingston-upon-Thames, who issued the postcard.

Right: Fleet number 459 was a 5-ton Saurer delivered in the spring of 1923 and is pictured here engaged in carrying a couple of storage tanks. These formed part of a batch of six which were delivered to Cromer, Southwold, Newbury and Yeovil, each being 12 feet in diameter and 10 feet high, and weighing 3ton 15cwt. Features of the Saurer were its original quality and powerful engine brake, and in this photograph the deep fish-belly of the chassis frame can be made out, whilst it has a hinged front towing eye for trailer shunting, and an ample rear sprag, so useful when starting on a steep hill when loaded. Although the machine has only a canvas roof and slide curtains for the crew, it does boast both headlamps and side lights.

Top right: An insight into the workings of a 1920s loading bank can be obtained by this photograph of a Pickfords depot somewhere in the London area. Lined up for loading is a mixture of vehicles including an open horse wagon, a lighter covered horse van, an open Foden steam wagon and a vehicle with hoops and sheet to cover the load. No doubt the staff are aware of the various items that are scattered about the loading bank — it cannot be as haphazard as it appears. Most of the goods are in heavy wooden crates and boxes, but the occasional basket hamper and barrel can be seen as well as some unpacked items of cane furniture. Note the sturdy little wooden 'desks' where the checker handles the paperwork; that early form of mechanical handling, the sack truck, is much in evidence.

Middle right: Some idea of the varied fleet employed on deliveries during the 1920s can be gauged from this photograph taken at an unidentified location. On the left is one of the 4-ton Tilling-Stevens petrol electrics with boarded tilt bodywork; next is a 1923 Leyland 4-tonner with hoops and a loose sheet for the load, while next to that is a 5-ton Saurer No.362. At the extreme right is a 5-ton Foden wagon of 1913 which has an open, fixed sided body.

trailers at docks and markets. A Caledon six-wheeler appears in the list, as do a couple of S&D low-loaders. Then we find two Fowler road engines, taken over with the London Traction Haulage Co., originally at Crane Grove, Holloway, later the LMS goods yard at Holmes Road, Kentish Town.

A surprising fact was that very few electric vehicles appeared in the Pickfords vehicle roster, although some were tried for meat delivery around the Great War period. Carter, Paterson & Co. had quite a number in their fleet for local deliveries, a sphere which suited the electric very well. What is more surprising is that out of the four directors of the General Vehicle Co. Ltd. of Birmingham, three were Pickfords men, namely O.H. Smith, James Paterson and W.J. Elliott.

One major job carried out by Pickfords which interested the trade press, was the removal of the entire AEC factory from Forest Road, Walthamstow to its new home at Windmill Lane, Southall in 1927.

The job commenced on January 31st when a Knox articulated low-loader delivered a Ransomes & Rapier 5-ton petrol-electric mobile crane to Walthamstow, and left shortly after with the first load of machinery.

The task of removing the 10,000-tons of machinery and stores was scheduled to be carried out over three months, during which time production was kept going partly by using new machinery which had been installed at Southall prior to the move.

The old factory at Walthamstow was located on three floors, and so much of the equipment had to be lowered on to the vehicles. Unloading at Southall was simplified by virtue of the fact that production facilities were located at ground level. Pickfords were responsible for all dismantling and fixing of machinery.

Much planning had gone into this major operation, and a route was adopted between the two locations which covered 19.9 miles, and drivers were advised to keep to it.

Pickfords did not get involved with moving any of the AEC staff, for the company had designed special large six-wheel double-deck buses, which carried no less than 104 employees on the daily trip between the two locations. These buses were the forerunner of the famous LGOC LS London Six type, which entered service shortly after the factory move.

In the late 1920s the French-built Latil tractor was tried, and was found to be ideally suitable for handling drawbar trailers on dock work and meat haulage. Some were used for handling the lighter type of special haulage tasks, where the more normal rigid vehicle was at a disadvantage because of space or manoeuvrability.

One or two more Scammells joined the fleet, which at this time was largely based on Saurer and Leyland for the heavier chassis, with Morris

Below: Although not as fine a photograph as those showing vehicles when they are new, a roadside photograph such as this does provide us with a contemporary view of period long distance operations. This Liverpool-based Saurer is pictured en route to London one cold and frosty morning, proving that removals were carried out without recourse to using the railways although lift vans are being used on flat vehicles. That on the trailer is covered by a sheet indicating that perhaps the van was not water-tight, and another sheet can just be seen behind the cab, where it would appear to be protecting a large item of furniture that was perhaps too large to fit into the van.

Right: As part of the contract fleet of the day, this Morris-Commercial is lettered for service with Boord & Son Ltd. who describe themselves as 'Distillers, Wine & Spirit Shippers' with an address in Tooley Street, not far from the headquarters of Hays Wharf Ltd. The high, fixed sided body is fitted with a drop tailboard, and the short framework for the tilt sheet at the front serves to help protect the load from the weather as well as providing anchorage for the sheet itself, which was then thrown back over any large loads. The location is probably Long Lane depot in the days when a large part of the transport fleet was still horsedrawn. A stable can be seen to the left, while above can be seen the walkway for the horses stabled on the upper floor.

Middle right: During the late 1920s the company secured a contract to supply vehicles for the Home and Colonial Stores, a multiple grocery chain. Four of these Shelvoke & Drewry low-loaders with extended wheelbase were added to the fleet, they being employed for moving loads of empty packing cases. With a wheelbase of 14ft and a body 20ft long they were ideal for this type of work, and the small diameter wheels made for a low loading height.

Bottom right: Latil tractor No.876 was a TL type placed in service in May 1927, painted in the colours of Hays Wharf, and was one of a batch of similar vehicles acquired for a variety of tasks within the Hays Wharf group operations. The scene appears to be the yard of Tower Bridge Road depot, judging by the high bar above the gateway, and the fact that the road outside is cobbled and has conduit type tram tracks.

and Bean being specified for the lighter transport jobs. One or two Fords, a Thornycroft, a Vulcan and a few W&G appear during 1928-29, plus a batch of Saurer 5-tonners for the new Multiple Shops department.

Into 1930, and diesel-engined Saurers appear on the books, followed by the well-publicised acquisition of the Fowler road engines and Scammells of Norman E. Box, the heavy Hauliers. This last takeover gave Pickfords two valuable new locations at Manchester and Birmingham, together with the necessary equipment, staff and management to make great strides in the field of heavy haulage, and it all came for £21,643 according to a contemporary report!

N.E. Box had a great reputation for the movement of heavy and awkward loads, and was currently enjoying a great increase in business, by virtue of the expansion of the national grid. This demanded expert handling of the many heavy items of electrical equipment being installed in the new power stations then being established.

About this time the new, lighter Leyland 'Badger' was being added to the fleet, complete with van bodies for furniture work or as platforms to take the lift vans if required. By today's standards they appear rather over-engineered, for they were rated as 2½-tonners, but household removals does not require a heavyweight chassis, so they were adequate until something better was to be developed a few years hence.

A batch of Commers was purchased early in 1931 as part of the booming Goods Service, more Leyland 'Badgers' were taken on for removals, and a handful of Karriers joined from the takeover of Woods of Altrincham. Another new marque appeared in the vehicle register — Mercedes Benz, but these might have been acquired in order to study the newly-arrived diesel engines.

Shortly, some oilers from Southall join the fleet, and AEC are not slow to advertise the fact. Multiple Shops add a batch of Ford 2-tonners to their operation, and a few Morris-Commercial six wheelers are in use with Removals and Multiple Shop departments.

The Goods Service is expanded and named the London Suburban Goods Service as a direct rival to Carter, Patersons' Home Counties Express. A new bodyshop is established at Riverside Road, Summerstown, and known only to a few, talks continue between Hay's Wharf Cartage and the railways about a possible takeover.

As things turned out, a significant decision was made in mid-1933, by the purchase of the first Bedford 2-tonners for the Suburban Goods Service, operating from Long Lane. They were also tried in the removals fleet alongside the Morris-Commercials currently in use. Others were allocated to duties with Hay's Wharf Cartage and Multiple Shop Deliveries. New standards had been established, which were to last for at least two decades.

Above: This novel way of moving a steam bucket excavator without the use of a trailer, is shown in an illustration taken from one of the many publicity booklets issued by Pickfords to advertise their services. This particular booklet dates from 1930 and publicises the Heavy Haulage department, but what makes it particularly interesting is that it was produced with a German text, evidently in order to induce mainland European manufacturers to engage Pickfords for the delivery of any heavy or large loads destined for this country. In this instance the Ruston excavator is being handled by one of the Fowler road locomotives of the London Haulage Traction Co. which was acquired by Pickfords in the 1920s.

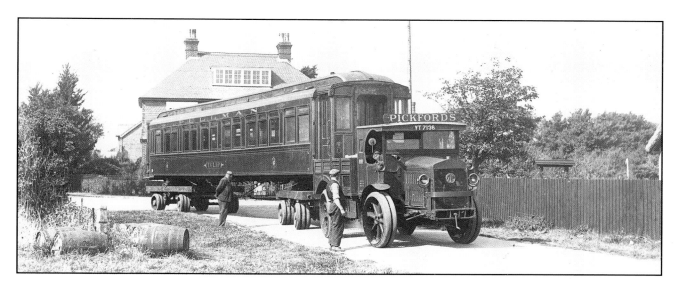

Top and middle right: After their experience with the early American Knox tractors, Pickfords had Scammell, Saurer and Latil tractors employed in the heavy haulage department, all being used for a variety of tasks as appropriate. No. 897 was one of the earlier Latils of the solid tyre era and is shown here handling the movement of 'Tulip', a Pullman railway car, from Selsey railway station to the beach nearby in 1930. The French-built Latil gained an enviable reputation as a useful machine for all kinds of towing, winching and haulage tasks with its all-round steering, traction and braking, aided by adequate gearing and twin-tyre equipment. The lower photograph shows the vehicle, suitably bedded-in for the winching operation with the mate, braced against the anchor, keeping a grip on the wire rope from the vertical winch spindle, while the driver keeps a watchful eye through the tiny cab rear window.

Right: The heavy snowfalls which occurred during the winter of 1927/1928 showed the need for some mechanical means of snow clearance, if journeys were to be completed within reasonable time. Pickfords engineers fabricated a bow-shaped steel blade and affixed it to the front of Latil tractor No.897. the V-shaped fabrication was some eight feet wide and almost as high, and its leading edge was supported on an old Tilling-Stevens wheel to keep the blade clear of the ground. It was tried out on roads in Kent and proved effective in forcing a route through drifts up to six feet deep.

Specification and Price List
of the
7/8-Ton Saurer Chassis Type 6BLD
fitted with
Saurer Heavy Oil Engine

One of a fleet of over 100 Saurers

Saurer's Sales and Service Branch House for the British Empire
THE SAURER COMMERCIAL VEHICLE CO. LTD
21 Augustus Street, Albany Street, London, N.W.1

**DESIGNED AND BUILT TO HAUL TRAILERS
WITH A 7/8-TON PAYING LOAD
THIS CHASSIS WILL SAVE UP TO 75% OF YOUR PETROL COSTS**

Left: Fleet No.993 was one of the heavier type 6BLD Saurer, which embodied the makers six-cylinder diesel engine, shown here on the front page of the 1929 catalogue. The brochure says that it was "One of a fleet of over 100 Saurers", and Pickfords had been using them since 1921.

Below: No. 1016 was one of the smaller Latil tractors kept at Tower Bridge Road for a host of the lighter indivisible loads which Pickfords handled with regularity. Being so highly manoeuvrable, the little tractors were ideal for handling the smaller items such as engines, boilers, transformers, winding gear, and as in this instance, small boats. As driver Green steps down from the cab, the crew prepare the boat which will be floated off with the rising tide.

Right: Eric, a 65-ton whale was transported from the Royal Albert dock to Olympia by Pickfords in December 1931 for exhibition at Bertram Mills' Circus over the Christmas period. The huge water tank used for carrying the whale was actually an oversize American railroad boxcar complete with underframe, and was successfully carried on a pair of short two-axle trailers with bolsters, towed by one of the ex London Traction Haulage Co's. traction engines.

Right: The 1930s saw the continuation of the Leyland marque in the Pickfords fleet with the introduction of the 2½-ton 'Badger' with either pantechnicon bodywork or as a flat as shown here. The detachable liftvan was still widely used in the removal business and the one carried by this vehicle still retains the roof boards which were so useful for the casual items which could not be accommodated within the van itself. Note the way in which these boards have been carefully recessed around the lifting eyes at the top of the iron slings which carry the weight when it is lifted by a hoist.

Left: The large fleet of Saurers used by Pickfords for their general haulage and removals departments, was followed by an almost comparable fleet of Leyland 'Badger' chassis with van bodywork. This tasteful Leyland advertisement of 1932 was one of a series issued by the vehicle manufacturer to underline the preponderance of household names carried by the Leyland marque.

Below: One of the highlights of the 1931 Commercial Motor Show at Olympia, was this diesel engined six-wheeler exhibited on the British Mercedes-Benz stand. This NK56 'Hercules' 10/12-ton model was powered by the makers 85bhp six cylinder engine, and was carried on 13.50x20 single tyres all round. The special design of all-metal insulated bodywork was by Duramin Engineering, and featured a patented overhead endless chain system whereby the meat carcasses were hung from the chain which ran round the body. Thus the whole weight of the load was supported by the roof of the vehicle. The drive shaft for the chain system can just be seen above the cab roof. This massive machine was operated by the Meat Department of Hay's Wharf.

Above: For some enthusiasts of heavy haulage, nothing can surpass the sheer power and magnificence of a pair of Fowler road locomotives as they go about their business in a unique fashion. Here we see 'Vulcan' and 'Atlas' in the livery of Norman E. Box Ltd., about to embark on a journey with a piece of outsize electrical equipment from the works of Metropolitan Vickers. This pair of engines formed part of the Norman E. Box fleet of six such machines which passed into Pickfords ownership in 1930.

Below: For many years the basis of the Heavy Haulage department was the Scammell, epitomised here by this 1931-model 40-ton machinery carrier loaded with an electric stator well supported with wood packing. Features of this period were the electric headlights with oil sidelights and the 'windows' in the bonnet sides through which could be seen the legendary Scammell 7-litre four-cylinder petrol engine.

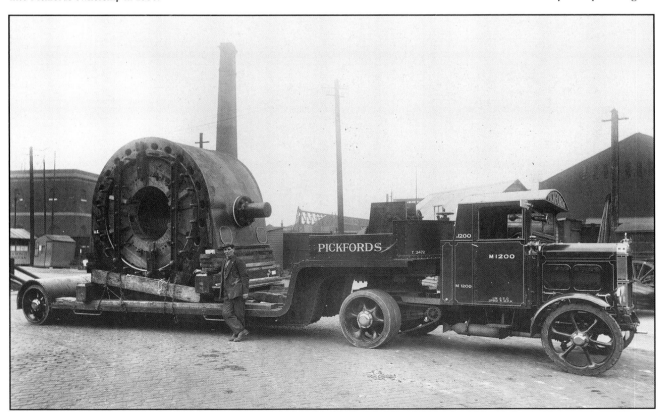

Left: Pictured at Victoria Southern Railway station during the 1930s is this Morris-Commercial C-type lettered for Continental Express Ltd. who were a firm dealing in cartage to and from continental Europe, and using the cross-channel service of the SR for some of their operations. This vehicle would have been based at the Long Lane Contracts depot. The roundel on the cab door carries the legend 'Licensed by HMH Board of Customs' indicating that Continental Express had been approved by HM Customs to carry goods under bond, and that its drivers were similarly 'bonded' and trusted with such goods. The photograph comes from one of the Pickfords brochures of the period.

Below: The use of models for advertising has been with us for a very long time, and many older readers will no doubt recall the use of model railway wagons containing pieces of coal in the windows of the local coal merchants. Pickfords realised the importance of having a three-dimensional model to supplement pictures way back in the days of horsedrawn vehicles, and a model of one of the old pantechnicons has recently been discovered. This photograph shows a display of five advertising models on the counter of the High Holborn premises, they being four Tilling-Stevens chars-a-banc and a Saurer household removals vehicle with detachable container. The removal van would have been destined for the office window where it would have taken its place amid all the contemporary advertising literature which included large framed photographs, posters and maps, which served to illustrate the wide coverage of Pickfords' business. The purpose of the other models was more functional, for they were issued by coach tour booking offices to show the actual seating layout, in order that passengers might better be able to choose the seat which suited them best. These fine scale models were the work of Mr. L. Gamlin of Teddington, and they featured every seat in detail as well as a fully working hood.

Right: The early 1930s saw the introduction of the first diesel or oil-engined vehicles as they were known at the time. A small fleet of AECs for trailer work were acquired, and this AEC advertisement of 1932 was used to publicise the fact that Pickfords "who possess vast motor haulage experience" have chosen to acquire no fewer than 20 of their chassis.

Important Transport Company places **REPEAT ORDERS** for **A.E.C. OIL-ENGINED LORRIES**

and now has on order and in operation

20

AEC

SOUTHALL

MOTOR VEHICLES

Messrs. Pickford Ltd. who possess vast motor haulage experience have proved the reliability and economical qualities of the A.E.C. Oil Engine. Having placed 4 repeat orders, they now operate and have on order 20 Oil-Engined A.E.C.'s. This popular 130 h.p. C.I. power Unit has undergone lengthy and exhaustive tests, and was only marketed after years of intensive research work. By expert designing, and the special selection of metals used in its construction, the A.E.C. Oil Engine in performance and weight, compares favourably with a petrol unit of the same power. Combined with these features is the low fuel consumption achieved. It will pay you to write for more details.

The popularity of A.E.C. Motor Vehicles for Overseas use is shown by the following countries where these vehicles are being operated with great success.
AUSTRALIA CANADA CHINA DENMARK GREECE NEW ZEALAND SOUTH AFRICA SOUTH AMERICA SPAIN STRAITS SETTLEMENTS SWEDEN

The Associated Equipment Co. Ltd., Southall, Middlesex
BUILDERS OF LONDON'S BUSES

Below: This rather magnificent vehicle is one of the six-wheel Morris-Commercial vans used in the Household Removals fleet during the early 1930s. It is the RD chassis type which was available in 12ft. 8in. or 14ft. 4in. wheelbase lengths and rated at just 2½-tons capacity. Quite a number entered service during the early part of the decade, but by 1933 the Bedford 2-tonner had appeared on the scene and old designs like this were facing obsolescence.

Left: The early 1930s saw a variety of Morris-Commercial types in the fleet, and they were to be found on Multiple Shop, Contract Hire and Household Removals. This example is a forward control version of the 3-ton 'Leader' supplied in August 1932, and with this sturdy furniture body it weighed 3-tons 15cwt. in unladen form; the chassis price was £485.

Below: New in April 1932, this AEC 'Majestic' was one of a batch acquired as replacements for some of the earlier Saurers, and was used on the Suburban Goods Service. It is pictured at the makers Southall works and the script on the radiator proclaims that it was fitted with the AEC oil engine, as diesels were known in those days. The trailer, with its solid rubber tyres, is obviously of earlier date, and carries one of the lift vans so favoured in that period. Note that the vehicle bodywork resembles a lift van with its angled crossboarding and lifting irons, yet it is securely attached to the chassis by means of U-bolts, so it was not intended that the body should be removed frequently.

Right: The mid-1930s saw a few of these little 3-ton Garner low-loaders enter service with Hays Wharf for general cartage duties, particularly with regard to dock and wharf traffic which involved the handling of large, but not necessarily heavy, packing cases. This was the RW3 model with a wheelbase of 12ft 6in and a body length of 20ft. Note that on the nearside the platform body is carried along the side of the vehicle cab in order that long loads of pipes, timber, etc could be accommodated.

Below: One of the most impressive vehicles employed in the Meat Cartage department of Hay's Wharf Cartage fleet, was this oil engined AEC 'Mammoth Major'. Pictured outside the Summerstown bodyworks in 1932, this vehicle was part of the company's effort to secure a part of the lucrative long distance meat cartage from Scotland to London.

Left: In 1933 Vauxhall Motors were proud of the fact that Pickfords now had 40 Bedfords in service. The 2-ton chassis was used for a variety of roles including a large batch for the Suburban Goods Service, and one of that fleet is pictured here at the Long Lane depot. Interestingly the photograph is a candid shot showing the yard in its working state, and the old granite setts have been rutted by many years wear from iron-tyred horsedrawn traffic. Other period features are the fully-opening windscreens so useful on hot days such as this, the diamond pattern 32"x6" tyres, and an unidentified radiator mascot.

Below: The Suburban Goods Service was a part of the Pickfords parcels carrying section created in 1932 in direct competition to Carter, Paterson & Co's Home Counties Express. These were some of the first Bedfords to be used in the fleet, and date from the middle of 1933. Bodywork is of the 'boarded tilt' type which means that the upper part of the body consists of dense canvas being tightly stretched across longitudinal boards and then given several coats of waterproofing.

Right: A scene from the early 1930s as one of the 1923-registered Saurer 5-tonners hauls an old single deck tramcar body out of the LCC works at Charlton, south-east London, into Felltram Way named after the General Manager, A.L.C. Fell. This was the time when the Kingsway Tramway Tunnel was being rebuilt to enable double deck tramcars to use it, and the old single deck cars were being sold off. The tramcar body is from an F-type, new in 1906, while over to the right stands one of the LCC B-class tramcars which had been withdrawn from service but retained for use as a staff tram. Note that the front towing bracket of the Saurer can be hinged up so that it is out of the way when the engine has to be hand cranked.

Below: One of the ex-Norman E. Box road locomotives, 'Talisman' , a Class B6 8bhp Fowler, built in 1925, is seen here shunting a heavy piece of equipment into position on the 32-tyred well trailer. According to the publicity board on the load it is a 15ft x 15ft cylinder made by Walmsleys (Bury) Ltd. and Bentley & Jackson Ltd.

for the St. Annes Board Mill Co. Ltd. of Bristol, and the date is February 1933. The use of wooden scaffolding on the new building, the old design of cement batching plant in the foreground, and the narrow gauge railway for moving materials about the site are worthy of note.

Under the Railways

The headline of the August 5th 1933 issue of 'Motor Transport' read: "Railways Buy Pickfords and Carter Paterson". The long negotiations, begun on July 4th 1929 when Guy Baxendale was on a river trip with officials of the LMS railway, had finally come to fruition, and the four main-line railway companies had gained control of the two largest road goods transport undertakings.

At the takeover, Pickfords still had 509 horses and 866 horse vans, in addition to 628 motor vehicles, so the mechanisation begun in 1903 still had a long way to go.

In December 1933 Guy Baxendale decided to retire from the business after 120 years of family interest in the company — another chapter in the Pickfords saga had begun.

Outwardly, the advent of railway control over Pickfords appeared to change things very little. For many years there had been co-operation at various levels, often with Pickfords renting railway premises or property, for its activities in provincial locations.

So far as the vehicle fleet was concerned, it was business as usual, there being no change in policy in that direction. 1934 saw more Bedfords in Pickfords colours, while Hay's Wharf took on a number of Scammell 'Mechanical Horse' articulated outfits for its activities. Some more AECs were bought and a few more small takeovers took place.

Pickfords started a regular trunk run on the old Manchester to London route in direct competition to the Bouts-Tillotson service. Whether this was begun with sound business judgement or just to please the railway masters is not known. The successful Bouts services with lightweight AEC box vans, was a thorn in the side of the railways, and Pickfords may have been used merely as a political weapon.

Whatever the reasons, the Pickford service was withdrawn after 15 months, allegedly because of a shortage of suitable vehicles. The railways were going to have to wait another 12 years before they could see Bouts-Tillotson toppled!

In May 1934 Pickfords took control of the Midland 'Red' Commercial Motor Service, which was the parcels service originated by the Birmingham & Midland Motor Omnibus Co. some 30 years earlier. This was rather a natural outcome of the railways takeover of Pickfords, and the subsequent re-organisation of the commercial services carried on by bus companies, in which the railways also had a financial interest.

As the service had been operated from the Seymour Street premises of

Right: The first Bedford trucks purchased by Pickfords were used on the new Suburban Goods service, aimed at breaking the almost complete monopoly held by Carter, Paterson & Co. Vauxhall Motors were quick to realise the importance of this new customer, promptly using the vans in advertisements as well as creating this colourful front cover picture for the December 1933 issue of the Bedford Transport magazine.

Below: The Dennis 40/45cwt chassis of the early 1930s was a very popular model for a wide variety of trades as well as municipal applications. It was also available as a six-wheeler and was rated at 3½-tons capacity. This 1934 model, with its single-tyred trailing axle and 975cu.ft. body, was allocated to the Glasgow branch of Household Removals, but like the contemporary Morris-Commercials of the period, they were superceded by the new lightweight Bedfords which were soon to become the accepted standard for removals work.

Pickfords, and the vehicles hired from them, it was rather an internal rearrangement than a major change of policy.

At the end of the year, one solitary vehicle was acquired which, in the years which followed attracted more than its fair share of attention. This was the Scammell 100-tonner, and No.1679 (BLH21) was a valuable addition to the fleet. It originally appeared in the fleet colours of Norman E. Box, for that arm of the company did have a long association with the heaviest of loads, they were still better known than Pickfords were in the north of England, and that is where the vehicle was based.

It's recorded unladen weight was listed as 11tons 6cwt, a figure that was to cause some problems much later, when it was discovered that as no trailer came with the tractor when bought, the tractor was weighed in solo condition. A trailer was duly ordered from Cranes, but the combined weight never declared, an oversight which came to light years after when the police brought a case against Pickfords, only to see it thrown out because it was brought under the wrong section of the law!

In August 1934, Pickfords began the operation of a new contract with Van den Burghs & Jurgens Ltd., for the transport of their Stork Brand margarine, from one of their two manufacturing plants at Purfleet, to the two London distribution points at Bow and Lambeth.

The fleet allocated to the new contract, was four Latil tractors and eight specially built drawbar box van trailers supplied by Cranes (Dereham) Ltd., and R.A. Dyson & Co. Ltd. This fleet level was sufficient to allow for the interchange of trailers which had been pre-loaded overnight at Purfleet, in order to achieve early morning delivery at the two distribution depots ready for transhipment to the delivery vehicles.

A brand new depot of some importance was opened in November 1935, when an H-shaped complex was erected on railway-owned land at Willow Walk, just off Old Kent Road in southeast London. As it was within the confines of the SR goods depot, it was assumed by some that this might be the start of a wholesale swing to depots being rail connected, since Pickfords was railway-owned.

The new depot was intended to relieve some of the pressure on the Long Lane premises, which had been in use for 69 years and was home to many branches of the business, such as Multiple Shops, Contract Hire, Hay's Wharf Cartage and the Suburban Goods service.

Below: The Hays Wharf Cartage side of the business was concerned with meat, shop deliveries, dock cartage, and general haulage, so the Scammell 'Mechanical Horse' fitted in well for work involving cartage work in congested city streets, markets, docks and railway depots. This is a 1934 6-ton vehicle with a dropside trailer that was suitable for a wide variety of goods. The location is not known, but judging from the general appearance it could well be one of the many railway depots in south London.

Bottom right: This Scammell 'Mechanical Horse' of the Removals fleet entered service late in 1934 being one of a batch of 3- and 6-tonners acquired at that time for a variety of duties within the Pickfords and Hay's Wharf fleet. The lashing rings on the trailer indicate that this outfit worked with the lift vans of the period, and the tiny hinged tailboard was more for show than practicality. One interesting, although hardly discernible detail, is the mounting of the tractor sidelights on hinged arms, secured by wingnuts — presumably moved outwards when the trailer was loaded.

Right: As part of the Parcels Service a number of light vans were employed in a bid to update the previously horsedrawn service. Various models in the Ford and Morris ranges were used as well as this little Raleigh tricycle van added to the fleet in 1934. Rated at 5cwt. capacity, the van was powered by a single cylinder air cooled engine of around 6hp., driving by way of a plate clutch and three-speed gearbox and chain drive. Earlier models retained the motorcycle type handlebars, but this model featured wheel steering. The Raleigh works were in nearby Nottingham, which might explain why the van was allocated to work in the Sheffield area.

Middle right: The Birmingham & Midland Motor Omnibus Company was very active in carrying parcels on its bus services, and added a fleet of vans to extend the service. A few years after the LMS and GWR railway companies obtained a shareholding in the company, the parcels service of Midland 'Red' as it was known, was transferred to Pickfords, who by this time was also under the control of the four main line railway companies. This 1934 Morris-Commercial was one of the vans allocated to the service, operating from Pickfords own Birmingham furniture repository.

With room for 143 vehicles, the depot covered four acres and was arranged to accommodate long-distance, dock, London collection and delivery traffic, segregated by means of numbered and named bays. Mechanical elevators could handle goods to a special storage area if delivery was not required immediately.

The old-established firm of Chaplins was added in 1936, this being a branch of the firm of Chaplin & Horne who, together with Pickfords, were engaged as agents in the old LNWR days. They had a long history going back to stage coach days, but not having been as fortunate as Pickfords, they had not expanded to the same extent.

In October 1938 the Carter, Paterson body-building subsidiary Express Motor & Body Works Ltd., was transferred to a large new site on the Great Cambridge Road at Enfield, Middlesex. As well as producing bodywork and painting for both CP and Pickfords, it was the base for the Benefit Tyre Company, another subsidiary set up to handle the extensive tyre requirements of the fleets.

As a tribute to W.J. Elliott, who had done so much to build up Pickfords from the early days of mechanical transport, the office block on the Southbury Road frontage of the complex was named Elliott House.

By the acquisition of Chaplins, Crouchers Ltd. and Shepherd Brothers Ltd., Pickfords was able to obtain a virtual monopoly of traffic to and from the Isle of Wight. In 1938 a new boat was commissioned for this ferry traffic, the MV Mount. Of 210 deadweight tons the boat was designed to carry up to eight standard Pickfords containers of either furniture or meat according to demand.

The approach of war in 1939 saw great changes in the company as one would expect. Many vehicles were acquired by the War Office, and the company headquarters was moved to Farncombe, Surrey for the duration. A vehicle rebuilding factory was established at Isleworth for the Ministry of Supply, and the Wholesale Meat and Provisions (Defence) Transport Association was formed in order to co-ordinate and run the wartime Meat Transport Pool.

The war period saw great changes in the operation of the vehicle fleet. Fuel rationing, air-raids, bomb damage, shortages of timber, steel and rubber, government directives, and the collapse of many established markets, all had their effect upon the company.

The parcels business was seriously curtailed, many of the staff left to join HM forces, vehicles and crews were switched to new and urgent jobs, the bodybuilding shops were tooled to produce parts of aircraft, and Pickfords vehicles could be seen carrying urgent war supplies and food to

Right: This view of the Pickfords 100-ton Scammell shows the vehicle at the Dereham works of Crane trailers where it had just coupled up the new trailer. The grey primer paint helps to emphasise the huge number of rivets used in the fabrication of the trailer sidemembers, and the steersman's hut and windlass type steering wheel can be seen. The scene is obviously a winter one, for the nicely tailored bonnet cover is in position and the driver has thoughtfully chalked 'MT' on it, as a warning to anyone that the radiator has been drained, for this was in the days before antifreeze.

Below: The joint parcels service which existed between Pickfords and Carter, Paterson & Co. was a well-publicised and large affair, but lesser known was the arrangement which prevailed in the Birmingham area with the Midland Red service. This purpose-built single-horse trotting van really shows a great advance over many of its contemporaries. Note that it is carried on steel artillery type wheels with the rear wheels braked, as in motor practice. The axles are very light in weight, and there is generous springing. The driver is positioned over to the offside and the van has electric lighting. Records show that the van body was 10ft. long. 5ft. 9in. wide and 6ft. high.

Right: When the Borough of New Windsor ordered a new Marshall road roller in 1935 and Pickfords carried out the delivery, the publicity department of AEC seized the opportunity to gain a photograph of the outfit in front of Windsor Castle. The vehicle in question was one of the diesel-engined AEC 0644 six-wheelers, which Pickfords heavy haulage classed as a six tonner!

many new, and often secret locations. The aircraft parts had to be moved to assembly aerodromes and later many landing craft as well as military vehicles were carried to ports of embarkation.

Because of its wartime activities, the company was able to acquire new vehicles during the war, but like everything else they were in short supply, so second-hand vehicles were acquired from wherever possible in order to keep the wheels turning. The smart new Bedford O-types supplied in the late 1930s were joined by the wartime versions, OXC, OXD and OWL, most of these being employed in the heavy haulage, food distribution and meat cartage departments.

With so many heavy items to be moved the heavy haulage section was allocated some new Scammell tractors, and in 1942 the first batch of the American-built Diamond T model 980 tractors arrived to supplement the hard-worked Scammells. Wartime allocations of new vehicles against MOWT permits also included ERF and Maudslay chassis, which were non-standard to Pickfords, but gratefully accepted by the fleet engineers who were faced with constantly repairing old vehicles in order to keep things moving.

Below: Pictured at the Pickfords bodyshops in 1935 is one of the handful of rigid low-loaders built on the Mark II AEC 'Mammoth Major' chassis. This unusual design was suitable for compact loads which could be accommodated on the 14ft. long well section, although in fact longer loads were often carried by raising them up to the wheelbox height by the provision of suitable packing.

In 1943 a start was made with transferring the Carter, Paterson business to the control of Hay's Wharf, which meant eventual amalgamation with Pickfords. Further alterations to the parcels business were made with a view to bringing it under one control, countrywide.

Even with the return of peace in 1945, the transport industry was still faced with shortages of almost everything. Rationing, allocations, permits and extended delivery, remained for a long while after the battles ceased. As far as possible, a vast vehicle replacement scheme was put in hand, with a view to fleet standardisation as far as was practicable.

By the time Pickfords and the associate companies were faced with public ownership, the fleet was undergoing a rapid modernisation, with many of the older, pre-war vehicles being replaced.

As in pre-war days, the bulk of the Household Removals fleet was on Bedford chassis with new O-types replacing many of the ageing WT-type 3-tonners. These were augmented by the lighter K- and M-type chassis, but most of these were destined for the Beans contract hire fleet. A few OSS tractor chassis were acquired for use with the large articulated vans used in the Removals fleet, while some were for the single axle trailer tanks of the Bulk Liquids fleet.

Right: On a cold and frosty day in December 1935 a convoy of three tankers set out from Birkenhead loaded with 7800-gallons of Mobiloil as part of a consignment of some 23000-gallons required for the lubrication of the turbines of the RMS Queen Mary. Suitably fitted with boards for maximum publicity, the convoy is pictured passing through Carlisle on its journey north, with a pair of Pickfords AEC 8-wheel tankers enjoined with a Commer in the livery of the Vacuum Oil Company.

Right: Much publicity was given to the vast new parcels depot established on railway property at Willow Walk, Bermondsey in 1935. This view shows the area between two of the 'legs' of the H-shaped layout, and must have been taken at a slack part of the day for just two WH-model Bedfords are backed-up to the bank on the right. On the opposite bank is a lone horsedrawn van which is prevented from being backed-up close to the bank by the three foot kerb provided as a safety stop for the motor vans.

Middle right: The Austin range of light vans for 1936 embraced three basic models of 5-, 7- and 10-cwt capacities, and this example in service with Pickfords Express Collection & Delivery Services, is the 10-cwt model. It was designated as the Light Twelve-Four, indicating that it used the four-cylinder engine which was rated at around 12hp. On the 8ft. 10in. wheelbase a body of modest proportions was only possible, for well over half the vehicle length was taken up with the engine compartment and driver's quarters. Noting that it was based at Sheffield, one wonders if there was any rivalry between the driver of this comfortable Austin, and the unfortunate driver of the rather primitive Raleigh three wheeler?

A few of the short tractor chassis were fitted up with ballast boxes and were put into service with the Meat Cartage department, handling the drawbar meat trailers between docks and market. Also used for meat transport was the medium wheelbase O-type chassis, as opposed to the longer wheelbase variety required for the removals department. Whereas meat is a dense and heavy load, household furniture and effects are light and bulky. Bodywork for meat cartage was usually of the insulated type whereas the removal vans had a single skin body with lashing rails down the interior sides.

Austins were quite well represented in the fleet at this time, with K2 vans turned out in the maroon of Cadburys or the red of SPD. The GV1 10cwt van was quite well represented, it being possible to see them in the liveries of Barnetts Bakeries, Ascot Gas Water Heaters, and the Welwyn Stores. There were quite a number of Austin K8 'Three-Way' vans in the fleet and most of them turned out in a variety of colours as specified by their hirers. The Polar Bear Laundry, Floris Bakeries, Civil Service Supplies Association and many other names appeared on the vans.

Scammells formed the basis of the Heavy Haulage fleet, with the addition of the wartime influx of the American Diamond T units, plus the batch of ex-military AEC 'Matador' 0853 types. The Scammells were of either drawbar tractor or articulated unit type and were mostly rated at 20- to 45-tons capacity.

As from January 1st 1946 the combined parcels operations of both CP and Pickfords were amalgamated to form the Carter Paterson & Pickfords Joint Parcels Service, which commenced operations with a stock of 1520 vehicles.

After almost three years this well organised operation was to form the basis for the establishment of the Parcels division of British Road Services.

As from January 1st 1947 the wartime Meat Pool became known as the Meat Transport Organisation Ltd., and soon the MTOL numbers were to be seen on all the meat traders vehicles, including of course those of Hay's Wharf and Pickfords. By this time the Removals part of the business had grown to 146 branches, 210 warehouses and some 400 vehicles.

In the same year the haulage part of Liverpool-based Garlick, Burrell & Edwards Ltd. was

Right: The Rootes Group range of Commer vehicles underwent a complete revamp in 1939 with the introduction of the Q models covering capacities from 15cwt. to 6-tons in rigid form. This example is an early 1939 15cwt. van and the lettering leads one to believe it was part of the Multiple Shops delivery fleet. The spoked artillery pattern wheels give the vehicle an old appearance, as do the tiny six-inch wiper blade and fully opening windscreen.

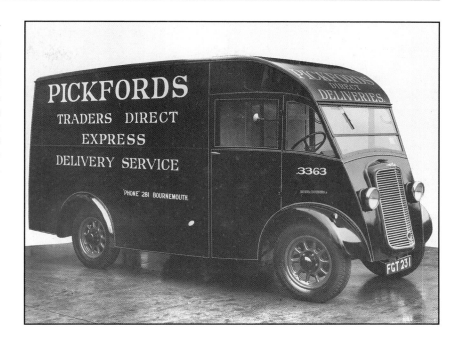

Below left: Bodybuilders are always keen to advertise that they build bodies for national fleets, but with Pickfords building their own vehicle bodies in the 1930s, it fell to the suppliers of the aluminium sheet and sections, the Northern Aluminium Company Ltd. to publicise the advantages of using their materials. In this 'Commercial Motor' advertisement of 1937, two types of Pickford vehicle are depicted: a Luton van for Removals and a box van lettered for the Collection and Delivery Services, both mounted on Bedford WTL chassis.

Below: Posed outside the bodyworks, this pantechnicon semi-trailer represents the state of the Household Removals during wartime, for it is a 1943 photograph and shows the additional white paint on bodywork and wings considered necessary for blackout driving. The Bedford WT tractor was new early in 1939 and has obviously not been repainted, the only additions being the white edge marking and the regulation headlamp masks.

transferred to Pickfords, and later some 25 contracts followed suit, including those with Cadburys, Ind Coope & Allsop, Wiggins Teape, GEC, Norman Foods and Union Cold Storage.

The company was deeply involved in meat transport, as well as general haulage and vehicle distribution, and the railways and Union Cold Storage Ltd. were major shareholders. As from January 1st 1935 the shares were sold to Pickfords, and they acquired a fleet operating mainly from Liverpool, but with other premises at Manchester, Glasgow, Leeds and Widnes.

Left: The two-ton Bedford WH model with integral bodywork figured largely in the Household Removals department, and sounded the end of the old era exemplified by the Leyland 'Badger' with a box body. Pictured leaving the east central London premises in Central Street is one of the 1938 WT model three-tonners which was the logical progression from the earlier two-ton models, before the introduction of the larger articulated type.

Top right: The Bedford three-tonners used on removals work came from the manufacturers in chassis/scuttle form, that is to say with just the radiator, bonnet, instruments and front-end sheet metal. The whole of the bodywork, from the windscreen back, was supplied by the bodybuilder. This view tends to emphasise the full-width cab which was necessary to accommodate the porters, but which finished up with no less than eight pieces of glass! Also worthy of note are the whitewall crossply tyres of the period, which appear to be of narrow section when compared with the low-profile fat tubeless radials of today. The odd-size headlamps are a carry-over from the restricted lighting of the wartime era.

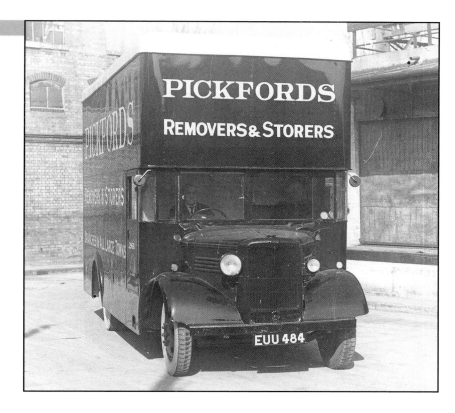

Below: Pictured proceeding at a steady pace over the moors, three of the Fowler road locomotives with a 117-ton hammer block collected from Sheffield. This was a wartime movement in 1941, and the first two engines have been equipped with masks for their minuscule headlamps while the third engine seems to have escaped attention. The squat Crane trailer is carried on 64 solid rubber tyres and on this occasion is utilised for carrying some of the coal supply for the engines, while the elderly living van for the crew brings up the rear.

Below left: Pickfords vehicles on contract to Whitbread & Co. the brewers, included a Scammell rigid 8 wheel tanker and this 1939 Bedford articulated tanker with Scammell automatic coupling gear. The tank had a capacity of 1440-gallons arranged in two compartments of 720-gallons each, and the large domes at the top concealed manways for access to the inside of the tank for cleaning purposes. The vehicle was used to carry beer in bulk from the main brewery at Chiswell Street, EC to bottling depots in the West Country and South Wales.

Left and below left: Over the years, Pickfords have been responsible for operating a number of unusual vehicles, including the AEC 'Crocodile' rigid low-loaders, the Holt tractors and a couple of McLaren oil engined tractors, one of which is shown here. The earliest model of tractor (1937) was of normal control layout with a sentry-box type cab at the rear, and was mounted on solid rubber tyres both front and rear, as per steam tractors of the period. This 1940 edition had progressed to forward control layout and could boast pneumatic tyres on the front axle, whilst retaining the period style giant solid rubbers at the rear, showing as they do the traction engine heritage of the vehicle. Powered by a McLaren five cylinder diesel engine rated at 95bhp mounted behind the cab, the tractor was capable of 10mph, and it weighed 12ton15cwt unladen, whilst there was provision for a further 4-tons of ballast if required. Provision for winching was by means of a drum attached to the inside of the offside rear wheel, and this could be engaged by a dog clutch when required, or disengaged from the road wheel by means of two detachable pins. Loads well in excess of 100-tons were within the capacity of the tractor, and one report put it as high as 190-tons. The design concept was interesting, being a hybrid between the old and powerful steam traction engines which had been the champions of heavy haulage since the beginning of the industry, and the more modern and easier controlled heavy lorry of the period. Although it remained in service until the 1950s, it was rather upstaged during the war by the introduction of the Diamond Ts. The photographs show the completed tractor outside the works of Charles H. Roe Ltd., who presumably built the cab and applied the finishing touches to this unique vehicle.

Above: The pressures of a variety of tasks during wartime proved the ability of road haulage to handle whatever it was asked to do. An example of this flexibility is shown by this Scammell articulated drop-frame carrier used in conjunction with a short drawbar trailer to carry a landing craft. The Scammell tractor was delivered just at the outbreak of WWII and is one of the mixed type embodying pneumatic tyres on the front axle while solids are retained for the drive axle. The headlamps carry the two types of masks required and a yellow triangular plate mounted on the front crossmember indicates that it was an authorised vehicle for electrical emergency work.

Below: Chaplins was one of the road haulage businesses acquired as part of the railways policy of buying up as much of the competing road services as possible, in the years following their acquisition of Hay's Wharf and Pickfords. This Bedford WH model of late 1935 shows the standard type of box van adopted for parcels and railway agency traffic by Carter, Paterson and Pickfords. Note that this vehicle carries the five-digit fleet number allocated in order to differentiate between the fleets of Carter Paterson and Pickfords when they were operating jointly.

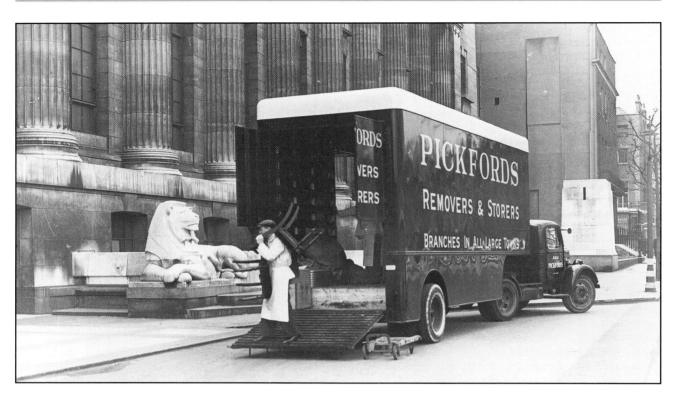

Left and below left: When the ultimate cubic capacity was reached with a rigid Luton-type removal van, Pickfords engineers looked toward the idea of articulated vehicles as being the next logical step in achieving even greater capacity with one vehicle. The design also broke new ground in that additional access to the load space was achieved by means of a door on the nearside of the van. When a moving job was booked for delivery to the British Museum, Pickfords publicity department was keen to exploit the occasion, and it was widely reported.

Below: This photograph is interesting, showing as it does Hays Wharf vehicles employed in more general haulage duties than that for which the group was better known. The three vehicles are a Mark II 'Mammoth Major' registered in Liverpool in the spring of 1937, a 'Matador' and trailer also registered in Liverpool, and a London registered Bedford 0-type artic of 1947. Although it is 1948 and the leading vehicles have lost their wartime white edging to the front wings, they still carry the Ministry of War Transport numbering system on the cab quarter panels.

Above: In a bid to improve the accommodation for three-man crews on removals vehicles, one of the first postwar Bedford OL chassis received this experimental forward control conversion. Official records show that it had "special type body over cab, with packers' seats, illuminated sign and extended chassis". The vehicle was allocated to the Head Office of Household Removals at Finsbury Park, but quickly relocated to the Felixstowe Road premises and disposed of in 1952. Note that the conversion to forward control extended to the body only, for the steering column, and therefore the driver, remained in the original position, thus rendering visibility rather limited.

Right: Seen in pre-nationalisation livery, this Bedford 0-type tractor was one of many which were converted to drawbar operation for the docks to market shuttle of meat cartage containers. In this instance the meat container is unusual in having side doors, most had doors at the rear. Note that the tractor carries a sheet on the nearside, a sure sign that it could be switched to carrying other traffic at any time.

Above: Many of the vehicles employed in the meat cartage business appear to have rather narrow bodies, the reason for this being that with the load hanging from the roof it is essential to keep the body width within the contact area of the tyres on the road. When cornering a hanging load can give a pronounced pendulum effect and cause the vehicle to overturn. The 1947 Bedford pictured here carries an MTOL number on its cab door, for all vehicles employed in the meat carrying trade were effectively controlled by the Meat Transport Organisation Ltd. This was an industry 'pooling' arrangement which had its origins in 1938, when a group of leading meat market transport operators were anxious to ensure an effective distribution service in time of war.

Below: The classic lines of the Scammell 'Pioneer' can be fully appreciated in this Scammell photograph of chassis number 6449 just before delivery in June 1948. Rated at 80-tons capacity, these tractors were used for most of the very heavy work in the 1950s, often working in tandem. The design had its origins way back in the late 1920s when Scammell produced their revolutionary design of highly articulated rear bogie which proved so useful in oilfield exploration and later, military use.

Below: In order to accommodate a gang of furniture porters which might be necessary at a large commercial removal, this pantechnicon trailer was built with a separate crew compartment over the swan-neck part of the body. The tractor shown has been attached purely for the photography session, for it was allocated to the Multiple Shops Department and normally operated with a smaller box van trailer.

Living with the Lion

The 1947 Transport Act gave the railways what they had been seeking for very many years — virtual control of the competing road transport industry. For the Act provided sweeping powers for the newly constituted British Transport Commission, to compulsorily acquire any haulage company, whose operations fell largely within the sphere of long distance operation.

As Pickfords was already controlled by the four main-line railway companies, it came as no surprise to find that the whole of the Hay's Wharf Cartage Company Ltd. together with its subsidiaries, of which Pickfords was undoubtedly the biggest, were acquired at the outset. So, in the first Monthly List of Acquired Undertakings published in September 1948, we find that Pickfords was listed under the reference of D2 as an Allied & Subsidiary Company of Hay's Wharf Cartage.

This single acquisition gave the new British Transport Commission set-up a great chunk of the contemporary heavy transport fleet embracing real heavy haulage, bulk tankers, household removals and of course parcels carriage in collaboration with Carter, Paterson & Co., as well as a sizeable contract hire fleet together with the old Beans Express part of the organisation.

The Meat Cartage department was impressive, although there were several other hauliers who had considerable shares in that particular sphere of transport, but at least the wide coverage of the country by the Pickfords business, gave the new masters more than a few bare bones, on which to hang many of the acquired undertakings which were to follow.

Pickfords became the Special Traffics Division eventually, for the company was not really involved with general haulage in any great degree, save for that part of the business that had evolved over the years with some of their customers, and partly through the takeovers of the firms such as Garlick, Burrell & Edwards.

It was not long after Pickfords became part of the new British Transport Commission that the vehicles of other acquired companies began to appear in their fleet. By this time the fleet numbering had reached the mid-5000 series.

For a while the number of premises showed an increase, for as a carrier's fleet was acquired so the premises came too. F. Short of Bath came into the fold early in 1949 with the vehicles being numbered in the 56xx and 57xx series. For a while the base remained at Bath, but gradually the fleet was allocated to other Heavy haulage depots and it was possible to see

Above: Scammell BLH21 was the second of the two 100-tonners and it came into Pickfords fleet on 17th November 1934, working mostly in the north of England from Manchester and Sheffield Heavy Haulage depots. In January 1951 it was to be seen delivering this diesel-electric locomotive to the South Bank site for display at the Festival of Britain, and the photograph shows the outfit being manoeuvred through St. Albans on its journey from the Newton-le-Willows. Interesting to note that at this time the road fund tax for the vehicle was just £145 per year!

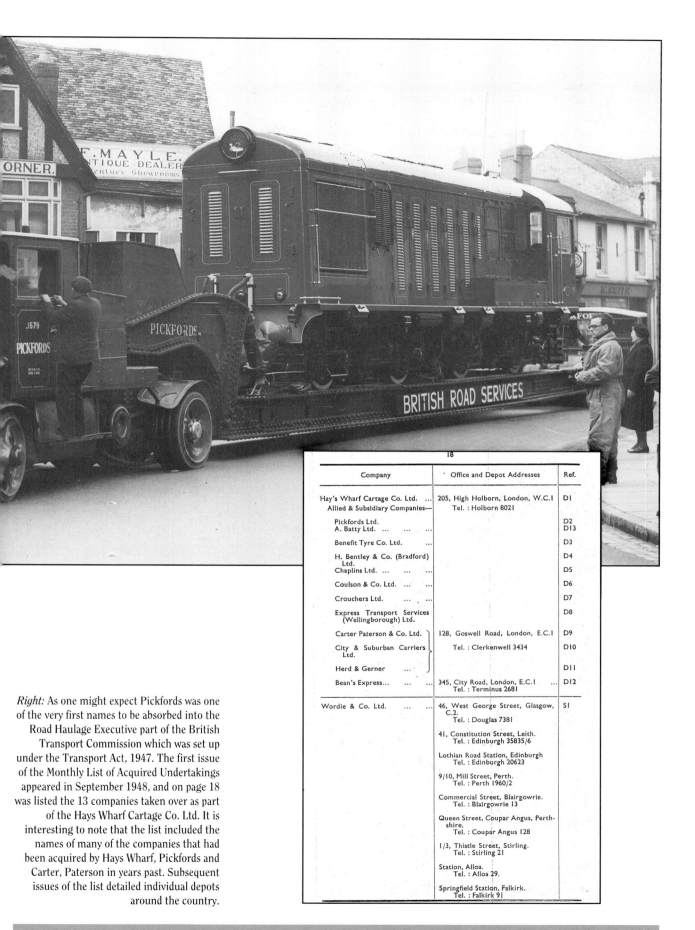

Company	Office and Depot Addresses	Ref.
Hay's Wharf Cartage Co. Ltd. ...	205, High Holborn, London, W.C.1	D1
Allied & Subsidiary Companies—	Tel. : Holborn 8021	
Pickfords Ltd.		D2
A. Batty Ltd.		D13
Benefit Tyre Co. Ltd. ...		D3
H. Bentley & Co. (Bradford) Ltd.		D4
Chaplins Ltd.		D5
Coulson & Co. Ltd.		D6
Crouchers Ltd.		D7
Express Transport Services (Wellingborough) Ltd.		D8
Carter Paterson & Co. Ltd.	128, Goswell Road, London, E.C.1	D9
City & Suburban Carriers Ltd.	Tel. : Clerkenwell 3434	D10
Herd & Gerner ...		D11
Bean's Express...	345, City Road, London, E.C.1 ...	D12
	Tel. : Terminus 2681	
Wordie & Co. Ltd.	46, West George Street, Glasgow, C.2.	S1
	Tel. : Douglas 7381	
	41, Constitution Street, Leith.	
	Tel. : Edinburgh 35835/6	
	Lothian Road Station, Edinburgh	
	Tel. : Edinburgh 20623	
	9/10, Mill Street, Perth.	
	Tel. : Perth 1960/2	
	Commercial Street, Blairgowrie.	
	Tel. : Blairgowrie 13	
	Queen Street, Coupar Angus, Perthshire.	
	Tel. : Coupar Angus 128	
	1/3, Thistle Street, Stirling.	
	Tel. : Stirling 21	
	Station, Alloa.	
	Tel. : Alloa 29.	
	Springfield Station, Falkirk.	
	Tel. : Falkirk 91	

Right: As one might expect Pickfords was one of the very first names to be absorbed into the Road Haulage Executive part of the British Transport Commission which was set up under the Transport Act, 1947. The first issue of the Monthly List of Acquired Undertakings appeared in September 1948, and on page 18 was listed the 13 companies taken over as part of the Hays Wharf Cartage Co. Ltd. It is interesting to note that the list included the names of many of the companies that had been acquired by Hays Wharf, Pickfords and Carter, Paterson in years past. Subsequent issues of the list detailed individual depots around the country.

the GL-registered ERF, Scammell and Maudsley units at Leeds, Bristol and Birmingham.

Fred Edlin of Leicester was another early acquisition and their premises formed an additional base for the Heavy Haulage department. Amongst the regular Scammell and ERF tractors in this fleet was an unusual Federal crane which became Pickfords No.5808.

At Bow in east London a bulk liquids haulier named Goldsmith was added to the fleet and this brought several new contracts into the operation. Pickfords had been in the bulk liquids business themselves for very many years, but in no way did they have a monopoly prior to nationalisation. Other tank hauliers such as Imperia and Lancashire Petrol Deliveries were soon to follow, the latter being a sizeable operation with bases at Bromborough and Urmston.

Other well known names were added to the rapidly expanding fleet during 1949/1950 including Gammon & Dicker Ltd. who had depots at Silwood Street SE16, Chatham and Tunbridge Wells, but only the meat haulage section was added to Pickfords, the remainder of the general haulage fleet being allocated to BRS.

Road Engines & Kerr was a firm specialising in heavy haulage in Scotland since 1932, although the two constituent companies went back to the last century. They were acquired halfway through 1949 and their Scammell, ERF and Diamond T tractors were instantly recognisable from the Glasgow registrations which they carried.

A batch of Scammells and Fodens came into the fleet via Eastern General Transport with bases at Ipswich and Kings Lynn, followed by some meat haulage Commer Q4 vans from Guest, Wood & Ling of Bath. A number of Scammells were taken over from the Nottingham-based R. Keetch & Son quickly followed by quite a number of heavy haulage outfits previously under the control of E. Box & Co. who were based in Liverpool, and were part of the Hauliers Ltd. group which included Beresford, Caddy & Pemberton of Tunstall, a firm of general hauliers, as well as Eastern General Transport.

A number of removal vans came from the Currie fleet of Newcastle-upon-Tyne, a company which, like Pickfords themselves, had been railway owned. A few vans came from Caudle of Birmingham, as did one or two from Airlandwater Transport of Bishops Stortford, another member of the Hauliers Ltd. group.

The Holdsworth & Hanson group was listed as being acquired very early on in the annals of the British Transport Commission, but their vehicles did not appear in the Pickfords fleet until the end of 1949, a year

Below: Pictured loading in Manchester docks is one of the fleet of trailer outfits operated by the Liverpool based part of the Pickfords general haulage department. Sharp-eyed readers will notice the Liverpool registration of this 1936 AEC 'Matador', for this part of the fleet originated with Garlick, Burrell & Edwards Ltd. a company which was built on carrying meat from the docks at Liverpool to nearby cold stores. Note the fleet number on this unit is M851 for these vehicles continued in the series originated by Garlick, Burrell & Edwards, even after the takeover by Hays Wharf Cartage, the practice continuing until the late 1940s.

Top right and right: From time to time the Heavy Haulage department was able to gain valuable publicity from particular haulage tasks which often featured the 'heaviest', 'the longest', 'the highest' — or some such qualification for being unusual. One such event was the movement of a 178-ton casting from the English Steel Corporation Ltd. works at Sheffield to Liverpool docks for shipment to North America. The task was put in the hands of three of Pickfords US-built Diamond T six-wheel tractors of the type which gained wartime fame as tank transporters, while the load was carried on a relatively new Crane 200-ton trailer which featured hydraulic suspension. Note that the Diamond T tractors carry an additional canvas 'cab' on the right-hand side, for with the vehicles having a left-hand driving position the driver was often blind to what was happening over to the extreme right, and an additional look-out man was necessary to provide assistance.

later. Some were listed as being acquired from J. Hanson, Milnsbridge, Grimshaw & Evans of Leeds, and Croft of Yeadon, all members of the group.

Early in 1950 the E.W. Rudd of Stratford, East London, fleet was absorbed, and this was quite significant for the company was an old and well established one in the field of meat haulage, as well as the better-known world of heavy haulage.

The meat cartage section was represented by Bedfords of both rigid and articulated types, plus a number of C15 ERF drawbar outfits. The heavy haulage section included a considerable number of Scammell tractors of 20-, 25- and 45-ton capacities plus a six-wheel 'Pioneer', while a

couple of the older (1930) Scammells had cranes permanently attached. Interestingly, the fleet included several of the Ransomes & Rapier petrol-electric mobile cranes which proved so useful in handling equipment when setting up exhibitions or fetching loads from inside buildings.

A number of Bedford and Austin 5-ton vans came into the fleet from meat haulier Bert Whiting of east London, and these were quickly absorbed into the Hay's Wharf meat cartage service and allocated to Poplar and other depots.

Parks of Portsmouth were responsible for adding a number of Dennis 'Pax' Luton vans to the removals fleet, together with an unusual — so far as Pickfords were concerned — articulated Dennis 'Horla'.

Northumbrian Transport of Gateshead contributed a handful of heavy haulage tractors in the shape of 20-ton Scammells and a DG Foden, while the first batch of Guy 'Vixen' removal vans joined the fleet from Robinson Transport from Norfolk, and Rainbows of Oxford.

Mid 1950 saw the acquisition of Mack's Hauliers Ltd., a sizeable fleet with headquarters at Silvertown E16, and branches at Salford and Southampton. The general haulage part of the business naturally went to BRS, but there was a large bulk tank fleet consisting of many Scammell articulated tanks together with Bedford, Dodge, ERF, Foden and AEC rigid tanks of various capacities. Unusual among the fleet were a couple of International K8 tanks as well as ex-military Fords. As with the Rudd fleet they were mostly registered in West Ham so stood out in the main Pickfords fleet, with their AN and JD registrations issued by West Ham County Borough.

Fred Cook (Transport) Ltd. of Hull operated a mixed fleet and the tanker part of it was brought into the Pickford operation during 1950. The majority of the tankers were DG Fodens of both six and eight wheel type, plus a few Bedford OSS tractors.

Premier Transport of Birmingham was a heavy haulage company which

Above & below: The post-war fleet included several ex-military types including a handful of AEC 'Matador' vehicles which saw service in the Heavy haulage and Engineers departments. With their four-wheel-drive construction they were eminently suitable for use as recovery and towing vehicles with the Engineers, and they were used as a tractor with drawbar trailers in Heavy Haulage operations or served as the ubiquitous tackle wagons backing up the Scammells and Diamond Ts of the period. In all, about a dozen of these 0853 'Matador' ex military machines were acquired from 1946. No. 4649 shows one of the vehicles as a recovery unit operating from Macclesfield Road, whilst No. 5305 was employed on heavy haulage duties at Tower Bridge Road.

Right: Nearing the end of its life with Pickfords Tank Haulage department, this 1939 AEC 'Mammoth Major' is of the Mark II variety but with the longer radiator fitted. The two-compartment oval section tank is probably of mild steel construction and suitable for a variety of loads: note the unusual crucifix style bearers beneath the tank. The front mounted exhaust silencer indicates that the vehicle complies with the current Petroleum Transport Regulations, and the long discharge hoses are carried alongside the tank without the need for enclosed boxes.

Below: The crew of this heavy haulage outfit have uncoupled the lead tractor and are preparing the oil lamps before they depart for their nights rest. Next morning they will be back to shunt the 74-ton press into the press shop of the Vauxhall Motors plant in the background. Lead tractor is Scammell chassis number 1931 a 1944 45-ton ballast unit, whilst the pushing Diamond T is a 980 model weighing over 14-tons and was obtained from the army at Slough in 1942.

added a few ERF, Foden and Scammell units to the fleet, but by far the most unusual were their Latil low-loaders with Boyes third-axle conversions, which dated from the early 1930s, one of which might still be languishing in a breakers yard.

A Guy 'Vixen' van from PX Ltd., the parcels carriers, appeared in the fleet, as did Scammells from Hine Brothers of Gillingham and Southern Roadways. A pair of Vulcan 6PF tankers came from National Road Haulage of Hull, whilst from Hepplewhite & Shaw of Sunderland came Atkinson and Scammell tractors plus the unusual in the shape of an International K8 flat.

One of the large capacity JNSN Luton vans joined the fleet from Reads of Peterborough, a pair of Seddons from Westmores on the Isle of Wight, and a brace of Scammell heavies from Isaac Barrie, the well-known Scottish heavy haulier. Weavers Transport of Worcester contributed Fodens of DGTU and FGTU types for heavy haulage operation, while Fordson ET6 and ET7 vans came from the fleet of W.S. Donaghy of West Hartlepool.

Whilst all these acquisitions were taking place, an accompanying increase in traffic was also recorded, so new vehicles were also joining the fleet in order to keep abreast of the expansion.

The Bedford OL types were still being added to the Household Removals fleet together with some for the Multiple Shop Deliveries. BSA motorcycles were being acquired for some of the less fortunate removals representatives, while others enjoyed the luxury of an Austin car. The contract hire and Beans departments took on new Austin K2 vans for painting in customers colours such as the green of Marks & Spencer and the dark blue of ICI, and Ascot Gas Water Heaters had some new Commer 3-ton and Bedford PCV 10cwt vans added to their contract.

In addition to the regular OL Bedfords and K2 Austins, the Meat Department also had new AEC 0853 'Matador' rigids and trailers allocated, and both Beans and Contracts were acquiring Austin K8 Three-Way vans for their work, Plessey being one such user.

The heavy haulage vehicles of Cliffords of Brentford were added early in 1951, together with a few vehicles from the large fleet of H. Burgoine of Hayes, Middlesex, the majority of whose fleet became Hayes Group of BRS.

A glance at just one page of the fleet list at this period is interesting, showing how it does the wide variety of vehicles being acquired. It includes AEC 0346 'Matador' (1946), Ford model Y (1934), Guy 'Vixen' (1950), Dennis 'Pax' (1949), Ford ET6 (1950), Bedford WTL (1936), JNSN (1948), Austin K4 (1947), Bedford OYD (1948), Albion KL (1937), Bedford OW (1943) and Ford 7V (1947). Altogether a very mixed bunch, and a nightmare for the stores to maintain an adequate supply of spares.

As nationalisation settled down, so there was a move toward standardisation in the fleets of both Pickfords and BRS, with vehicles being

Above: Pictured against the fine building of the Central Meat Markets at Smithfield is one of the short wheelbase Bedford tractor units for handling drawbar meat trailers. It is a 1942 OXC Model with ballast box which made up for the unladen weight of some 3-tons 18cwt, and it was garaged at the Poplar depot of the Meat Cartage department. The insulated container appears to be secured by just two chains toward the rear.

Bottom right: Not all loads had to be carried — some could be towed! A 1948 Scammell 20-ton ballast box tractor based at Park Royal, seen en route to the Clapham Transport Museum, with the Ipswich Corporation single deck trolleybus.

Top right: The company employed its own extensive vehicle workshops from the early days of mechanical transport and later moved into the sphere of actually building its own bodywork. In the late 1930s extensive facilities were built at Enfield under the name of the Express Motor & Bodyworks which was a Carter, Paterson & Co. subsidiary. This Albion chassis has been modified by the addition of a drop step at the rear, and with the body framing, cross-bearers, wheel arches and roof panels in position, it awaits fixing of the floor, body panelling, interior tie-strips, cab windscreen, doors, bulkhead and cab fittings.

transferred between the two with regard to traffic, type and use. One such instance was with the New Furniture division, where a considerable number of large vans were transferred from London groups of BRS to Pickfords for this work. There are even instances of chassis being acquired by Pickfords, allocated fleet numbers, and then transferred to the various divisions of BRS.

One of the largest fleet acquisitions was that of T.M. Fairclough, an east London carrier engaged largely on meat cartage, but with a fair amount of contract work also. Originally acquired by the RHE in April 1950 after lengthy argument, the 205 units were allocated to 72A Stepney group of BRS, most of the fleet subsequently passing to Pickfords meat department early in 1951.

The fleet was certainly a mixed one, from a 1928 Latil tractor through many Dodge, Morris, Bedford, Leyland, AEC, International, Maudslay, Scammell, ERF and Foden units, to the latest Bedford registered in January 1950. It also included a large number of drawbar trailers with insulated containers used on the docks to Smithfield Market transfer, a few of which were six wheeled!

Another meat carrier acquired was Matthews & Co. (Carriers) Ltd. who ran an assortment of Scammell Mechanical Horses and Foden DG tractors on dock work, with Foden and AEC rigids being used for journey work, often with trailers, plus a number of Bedford OSS artics. This fleet contained some quite old AECs, including a pair of 667 model 'Mammoths' dating from 1932.

A handful of heavy haulage outfits came from John Young of Glasgow including ERF and Foden tractors of around 25-30-ton capacity as well as EGG999 their model 980 Diamond T, which was sold to Robinsons in 1954. White of Hackney added some vans to the fleet, as did Perris Brothers of Liverpool with their mixed fleet of Dennis, Dodge, Austin, Albion, Bedford and JNSN units.

Another meat carrier acquired was E. Wells & Son of Rotherhithe, an old established haulier who once operated Foden steam wagons and Swiss-built Saurers, although none of these survived to see nationalisation. However Pickfords did take on some veterans from this fleet, including AECs of 1931, 1932 and 1934, as well as a bunch of International-McCormick road tractors dating back to 1929!

Still the acquisitions continued. Chesters of Nottingham; Al Sheppard of Willesden; Alfred Bell of Newcastle; Sunter Brothers; Marks of Harrogate; Beresford, Caddy & Pemberton of Stoke-on-Trent; J.W. Smith of Sheffield; J. Smith of Felling; C.S. Jones of Liverpool; Rogers of High Wycombe; Bert West of Barrow, and Ruddel of Potters Bar — all became part of Pickfords.

But the pace was beginning to slow. Not only had some 4000 undertakings been acquired by the RHE, but a General Election was on the horizon, and with it came a new government, new legislation and more to the point — denationalisation.

The Transport Act of 1953 laid the ground for the disposal of part of the assets of British Road Services, and of course Pickfords.

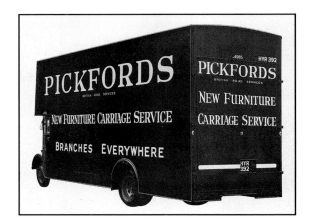

Below: A section of the business which saw great expansion during the period after 1948 was that of the New Furniture Carriage Service, for many small companies which specialised in this traffic were compulsorily acquired. This photograph depicts a Bedford OLAZ chassis with Enfield-built 1400cu.ft. pantechnicon body finished in the livery adopted for this service which includes, almost begrudgingly, the legend British Road Services, albeit in about two-inch lettering!

Right: The Engineers department was responsible, among other things, for the supply and maintenance of the vehicle fleet, and they had premises at Brixton, Summerstown, Tower Bridge and Enfield at various periods of their history. With such a large vehicle fleet the supply of tyres was a major item and the company set up its own Benefit Tyre Company for the supply and repair of them. Based at the Enfield facility this wartime Bedford OX artic van was used for the distribution of tyres to operating depots around the country. The vehicle was originally in service with Currie & Co. of Newcastle-Upon-Tyne, being acquired by Pickfords late in 1949.

Right: At the height of their popularity Bedford trucks formed a large proportion of the medium weight vehicles in the fleet, they being used in all branches of the firm's activities. This Vauxhall Motors photograph shows a 1948 OSS model tractor with Scammell automatic coupling in service with the tank haulage department. It is shown loading at the J. Lyons & Co. Greenford factory with a tank which has been taken from a rigid vehicle and mounted on a trailer frame which makes it unduly high compared with a frameless tank. Note the special holder for a wheel scotch on the nearside trailer frame.

Top left: A puncture is usually a straight-forward task with normal road haulage vehicles, but when a loaded articulated low-loader is involved the task becomes more onerous. Here a Heavy Haulage department Scammell has suffered a puncture to one of the tyres on the trailer and although it is quite accessible, the tyre repair fitter needs the assistance of the vehicle crew in order to safely jack and pack the trailer and the NCK bucket loader it carries. Luckily Biggleswade town centre provides enough space for the Marsham tyre fitter to do his job. Worthy of note is the wartime Bedford OB bus in the background, for it is operated by Tersons who were the Building department of Carter, Paterson & Co.

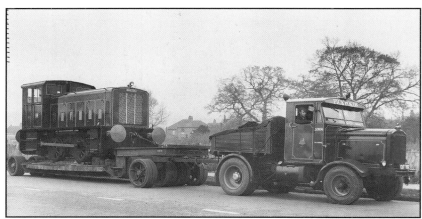

Middle left: The Scammell 20-ton, 25-ton and 45-ton tractors formed the backbone of British heavy haulage for very many years following the demise of the slower and heavier steam tractors. Many Scammells were to be found in the Pickfords fleet, especially after 1948 when many other heavy hauliers were taken over. Typical is this 45-ton ballast tractor of 1941 (CUT792) which joined the fleet in 1949 from Kinders Transport of Leicester.

Bottom left: Not all indivisible loads are very heavy — this one weighed just 6.75-tons! This silo was provided with triangulated supports at front and rear so that it could be suspended between two small bogies. Measuring 34ft long and 15.5ft in diameter when bare, the additional framework made it up to 49ft long for transportation, although the suspension provided a ground clearance of just six inches. The Scammell tractor in this instance was chassis number 6383 originally delivered to R. Keetch of Nottingham in 1947, passing to Pickfords in November 1949.

Right: The Heavy Haulage department acquired most of the serious competition by way of the 1947 Transport Act, and one of the best known was the fleet of E.W. Rudd of Stratford, east London. Here is one of their Scammell drawbar tractors complete with an old solid tyred trailer climbing toward the Highgate Archway. The Scammell is chassis number 1902 and entered the Rudd fleet late in 1943, it being rated as of 45-tons towing capacity with an unladed weight of almost 7½-tons.

Below: This fine photograph of a Scammell 'Pioneer' ballast tractor shows the livery adopted in the interim period between a company being acquired, and the vehicles being repainted in full Pickfords paintwork. Finished in Pickfords blue and complete with white lining, fleet number and the 'hungry lion' on the door, the old company name of E.W. Rudd is still perpetuated on headboard and body sides. This system did not continue for long, most of the acquired vehicles being quickly repainted in standard blue unless they were time-expired and were awaiting disposal.

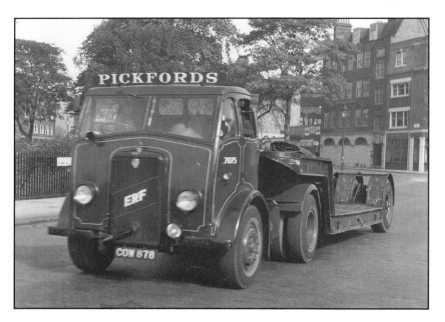

Left: Pictured running empty on Tower Hill, this ERF articulated low-loader is a 1940 vehicle acquired on 1st October 1950 from George Baker of Southampton. Rated at 15-tons, this C16 model No.1981 was based at the Stratford heavy haulage depot which was originally the home of another heavy haulage company, E.W. Rudd Ltd.

Below: Macks Hauliers Ltd. had a 200-strong fleet composed mainly of tankers, many of which were absorbed into Pickfords in June 1950. One of the 15-ton Scammell tractors was BAN11 seen here working on the Distillers Ltd. contract, and painted in plain green colour with no visible Pickford identity.

Above: For a while after nationalisation many of the ex Rudd Scammells continued in service still bearing the name of their previous owners, although carrying Pickford fleet numbers. Parked up for the night on the layby on the North Circular Road opposite the old Hendon Greyhound Stadium, is this solitary drawbar tractor of 1942 vintage, with a petroleum distillation column destined for one of the new oil refineries of the period. By todays standards the equipment looks decidedly ancient, consisting of a pair of 16ft long bolster trailers with long drawbars, the load being secured by just two single chains.

Below: Pictured outside the old depot of Coulson & Co. at Park Royal is this 1948 Foden DG tractor with knock-out axle low-loader trailer, in this instance carrying one of the old Ransomes & Rapier petrol-electric mobile cranes, which proved invaluable for handling plant within the confines of customers premises, or when installing items of machinery at exhibitions. The tractor was originally in service with Weavers Transport of Worcester, being acquired by Pickfords late in 1950. In the background towers the impressive brewery of Arthur Guinness & Co, established here in 1937.

Left: With a Luton extension which seemingly threatens to crush the cab, this voluminous van was in service with the New Furniture division of Pickfords in the days of nationalisation. The chassis is a 1951 Austin 'Loadstar' model, and the vans were often to be found in the back streets of east London, the area which was home to many of the furniture factories of the day.

Below: Pictured in brilliant sunshine at Smithfield Meat Market, this 1938 Leyland 'Beaver' with insulated meat container is lettered in the BRS Meat Cartage Service although numbered in the Pickfords special traffics scheme. Originally in service with T.M. Fairclough of London E.1. it was acquired by the Road Haulage Executive in April 1950 and passed, along with many of its stablemates, into the Meat department. The MTOL number on the cab door refers to the Meat Transport Operations Limited which carried on into the post-war period the work of the wartime service set up to handle all movements of meat under the direction of the Ministry of Food.

Top right: Although bearing a British Road Service headboard, the Meat Cartage Service was part of the Pickfords arm of the Road Haulage Executive, being classified as one of the 'Special Traffics', as opposed to general haulage. Much of the meat transport from docks to markets was handled by drawbar tractors such as this 1938 Leyland 'Beaver' acquired as part of the Fairclough fleet taken over in 1951.

Below: Scammell 'Pioneer' MLF22 was often featured in photographs showing heavy loads being moved during the 1950s. In this instance it is pictured on Millbank SW1 with one of the scaffolding-clad towers of Westminster Hall in the background. The load is one of the giant fractionating columns manufactured by G.A. Harvey and Co. of southeast London, for the new refinery of the Vacuum Oil Company at Coryton on the Thames estuary in Essex.

Left: Seen leaving the Camberwell premises of Samuel Jones & Co. Ltd., where it had just completed a delivery of hot liquid glue, is one of the Bedford S-type articulated tanks operated by the Tank Haulage department. These premises were later demolished in order to make way for a new development, but luckily the very colourful 'Butterfly Brand' trademark, at the top of the building, was saved and can now be seen on the local library building.

Below: For many years the Scammell reigned supreme as the mainstay of the heavy vehicles used by both the Heavy Haulage and Tank Haulage departments. Although being of the articulated layout, most were not of the readily detachable type, and a heavy jacking device or some form of frame was required to support the front of the trailer when it became necessary to uncouple the outfit. Nevertheless they were extremely reliable vehicles and much liked by their drivers, once the gate-type gear change arrangement had been mastered. Pictured here is a 1944-registered example being loaded with fuel oil at Dudgeon's Wharf, Millwall, while alongside is a more modern vehicle from the Crow Carrying Company of Barking which was an almost 100% Scammell fleet in its heyday.

Top right: Among the many AEC and Scammell tankers working from Bow depot of the Tank Haulage department in 1957 was this Atkinson L1586. It was originally ordered by Lancashire Petrol Deliveries Ltd., Manchester but before it could be delivered the company was nationalised, the fleet passing into the control of Pickfords on the 10th August, 1949. Being delivered in September of that year it received a London registration as part of the series issued to its new owners. With a two compartment, 3600-gallon stainless steel tank it originally carried fleet number 6134, later being renumbered M317 as seen here.

Middle right: The post-nationalisation Meat Cartage department vehicles continued in the Pickfords numbering system although they were turned out with British Road Services lettering. This Leyland 12B 'Beaver' joined the fleet in 1952 and is seen in south London after loading at Smithfield market. The insulated containers are of the usual pattern with roof eyelets for handling by overhead cranes and slings, and are secured to the vehicle by means of chains and turnbuckles.

Bottom right: Only the registration number gives a clue to the ownership of this 1952 Scammell articulated hopper, built for the transport of carbon black from Stanlow to Fort Dunlop for the manufacture of tyres. Unlike today when registration plates are of the reflective type, Pickfords vehicles used to have hand-written number plates, and the signwriter's characteristic hand could easily be identified.

Left: The Austin marque did not achieve such large numbers in the Pickford fleet as did the products from Luton. There were batches in use by the Meat Cartage department, some in New Furniture and several in the Tank Haulage department as this BMC-diesel engined example shows. This is the makers tractor version of the 701 model, which was rated at 10/12-tons capacity bringing a 2000-gallon tank within its grasp. In this view a Bow based vehicle is leaving the Esso loading facility at Hammersmith in west London.

Below: Making a right-hand turn after negotiating a low bridge, a pair of Scammell 'Constructor' tractors with the 200-ton capacity Crane trailer are pictured moving a Parsons transformer. This type of movement became common-place in the 1960s for Pickfords had some of the best crews and equipment, plus many years of experience in handling such jobs.

Above: The two main types of road tanker employed by the Tank Haulage department in the 1950-1960s are both shown here in this 1958 view of deliveries being made to Vinyl Products at Carshalton, Surrey. The Scammell on the left is making a delivery of heavy heating oil, whilst the AEC 'Mammoth Major' is dispensing vehicle fuel to the factory storage tank.

Below: Pausing at Houghton-le-Spring, County Durham in April 1958 is this Scammell 'Constructor' hauling a rail-mounted Coles crane which was enroute from Sunderland to Earls Court. Assisted by a ballast tractor version of the 'Highwayman', the load sits easily within the well of the Crane trailer, and the whole outfit seems rather an overkill, for the load weighs around 56-tons only.

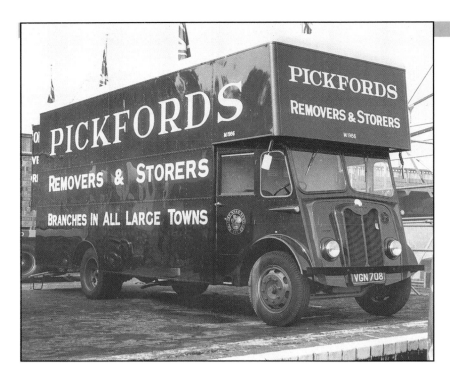

Left: Pictured at the joint BR/BRS Battersea Wharf display of transport and vehicles in 1958, is one of the Guy 'Vixen' Luton-bodied vans operated by Household Removals. Based on the makers 4-ton chassis this type of van superceded the previous standard removal vans which used the Bedford chassis as their base. Several variations of bodywork appeared on Guy chassis, the one shown here having the later type of moulded-grp front end which incorporated the dummy radiator shell and scuttle. Earlier models had used the normal production Guy cast aluminium radiator surround and a sheet metal front end.

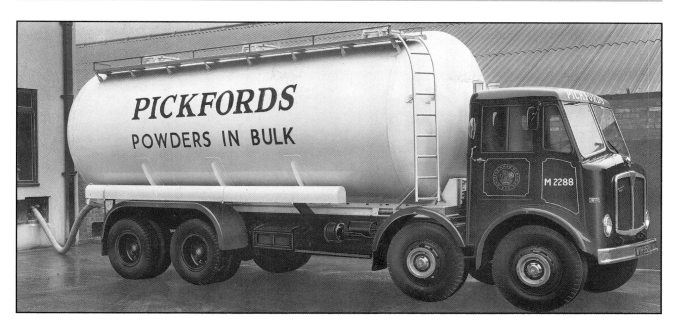

Above: Whereas tankers had historically always been associated with carrying liquids in bulk, the demand for the transport in bulk of gases, powders, pellets and granules, had led to the widespread development of tankers for these commodities. Pickford were well placed to take a share in these new traffics and several different types of vehicle joined the fleet. This AEC 'Mammoth Major' of 1962 carried an 1100cu.ft. aluminium tank built by Carmichael and Sons (Worcester) Ltd. which was tipped for discharge but had a low pressure air system to assist with clearing the load. Although there are three loading hatches at the top of the tank it is of the single compartment type, the three hatches merely helping to load more quickly as well as assisting with spreading the flow of the powders.

Below: This photograph of one of the two-stroke diesel engined Commers acquired in the late 1950s, serves to show the great emphasis on chromium fittings of that period. The enormous twin silencers were an outstanding feature of Commer vehicles fitted with the TS3 opposed piston engine and on tractors such as this there was the added problem of space to accommodate such bulky pipework. This vehicle was to be exhibited at the 1958 International Commercial Motor Show at Earls Court.

Left: Pictured at the Watford works before delivery, this 1958 example of the Scammell 'Constructor' clearly shows some of the front-end detail often missed with road-going shots. The cycle-type front mudguards are useful in that they can be of much smaller size than the fixed bodywork type, and as they are mounted direct on the axle can be fitted close to the tyres — very necessary with the oscillating front axle layout. A substantial front towing bar has three positions for central and offset connections, and the low-mounted lamps have stout grills to protect them from wandering drawbars! The mirror mounted atop the radiator gives the driver a view of the towing bracket, three palm-couplings are provided for the air brake system and to the nearside is positioned the fairlead for the vehicle winch cable.

Left: One of the several tankers on contract to Fina Petroleum Products Ltd., this 1956 AEC of the Tank Haulage department is pictured just before entering service. The two compartment, 3700-gallon tank is fabricated from mild steel with an aluminium cladding over a layer of insulating material. It seems that someone has rather overdone the white paint!

Bottom left: During 1964 this bulk powder tank was added to the fleet engaged in this fast expanding facet of bulk transport. Although of straight-forward design and layout, it did possess the unusual feature of carrying its own power plant in order that discharge might take place when the tank was delivered and left without the towing tractor. Constructed so as to conform with TIR regulations it was envisaged that deliveries to continental Europe might take place without its normal Atkinson tractor unit and another vehicle might not have compatible power connections. Based on the Bonallack Pneumajector system the tank was available for a variety of cargoes, it having a capacity of 1050cu.ft. with a payload of around 14-tons.

Above: Pictured inside the Heavy Haulage depot at Spindle Point near Manchester is this 1937 Foden timber tractor which proved itself useful for many tasks involving the winching of loads into position prior to loading. The fairleads of the winching gear can be seen between the rather minuscule headlamps positioned just above the front towing eye. Note also the old style of Foden radiator positioned just behind the cab, for this type of vehicle had its power plant mounted across the chassis frame behind the cab, hence the smooth front to the DG style cab which was devoid of the usual Gardner engine.

Below: The Guy 'Vixen' removal pantechnicons began to enter service from the early 1950s, ousting the Bedford from their premier position in the fleet, which they had held for around 20 years. Guys had never been entertained for this work, until many of them were taken over from smaller operators during the nationalisation period and their value for body capacity on a forward control chassis realised.

Above: M3099 was one of a pair of drawbar versions of the normal control Atkinson heavy haulage tractors specially built for Pickfords in 1963. Designed for a gross train weight of 35-tons, these tractors featured the Gardner 150bhp engine as usual, but final drive was by means of a spiral-bevel double-helical gear rear axle. A 6-ton ballast box with space for gear stowage assists with traction, cycle-type mudguards are fitted to the front wheels and twin 40 gallon fuel tanks are fitted.

Below left: As the Removals fleet was expanded and modernised during the 1930s, the old type lift vans were gradually phased out of this work, although they remained as part of the Meat Cartage fleet much longer. However, until the advent of the ISO stackable containers in the 1960s, the old style lift vans were indispensable for services to off-shore islands and countries overseas. This is a postwar example and is pictured on a British Railways Southern Region Austin 'Loadstar' articulated outfit, probably bound for the Isle of Wight.

Right: Pickfords favoured the elliptical-section tank for most of their rigid tankers, whilst the majority of the articulated tanks were of cylindrical section for pressurised loads. This 3600-gallon, three compartment mild steel tank was mounted on an AEC Mark V chassis, and is shown prior to licensing. Mild steel tanks can be used for a variety of cargoes, so long as there is adequate cleaning of the interior before being switched to a different load. Steam cleaning is the most common form of cleaning, and it is usually the responsibility of the unloading point to carry out the cleaning before the tank continues to its next load.

Right: Seen here on the stand of Atkinson Vehicles at the 1962 Commercial Motor Show at Earls Court, is one of the batch of Atkinson tractors of the Heavy Haulage department. These 40-ton capacity units, designated as SBT746XA, were aimed directly against the niche in the market held by the venerable Scammell. Pickfords took a number of Atkinsons eventually running both bonneted and forward control types, in both four and six wheel versions, with some operating as articulated units and others as drawbar tractors. This particular model was even fitted with cycle-type mudguards over the front wheels even though the axle was suspended by twin springs and did not oscillate as did the Scammell. The cab used was the normal Atkinson grp affair as used on the main range, while the bonnet was another grp moulding grafted on and given a rather bland frontal treatment by comparison with the classical aluminium type radiator surround of the current standard truck range.

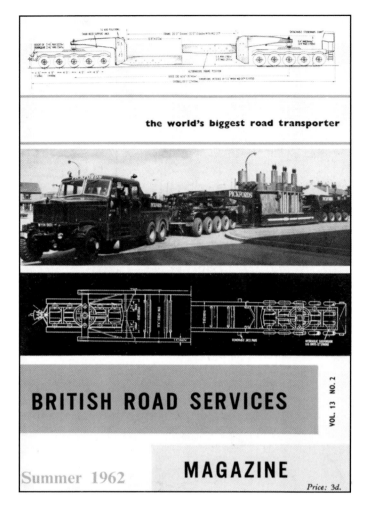

the world's biggest road transporter

BRITISH ROAD SERVICES

VOL. 13 NO. 2

Summer 1962

MAGAZINE

Price: 3d.

Left: Although Pickfords was part of the British Road Services organisation whilst being under the control of the Road Haulage Executive, it tried to distance itself from the everyday road haulage operations of BRS. However, the BRS Magazine was supposed to appeal to all members of the road haulage side of the RHE, so it is not surprising to find that the front cover of the Summer 1962 issue was given over to publishing the recently-delivered Crane 300-ton trailer.

Below: Seen snaking through traffic in the historic town of Warwick is one of the unusual Leyland 'Beaver' ballast box tractors with a special export trailer made by the Eagle Engineering Co. Ltd. The trailer houses a mobile generating plant and is carried on four axles arranged in two rows with a single heavy leaf spring mounted between each pair of twin tyres.

Above and right: The Household Removals branch at Wealdstone in Middlesex must have been full on this April night in 1962, for one of the Thames Trader vans has had to park in the nearby British Railways yard. For a brief period a number of these Ford vans were used in the fleet, as well as a smaller number of tractor units with Scammell-type couplings.

Slimming Down & Building Up

The passing of the Transport Act of 1953 marked the end of the acquisitions by the BTC, and by means of the Disposals Board which was to be set up, actually reversed the trend of expansion of the RHE. The intention of the Act was to sell off some 35,000 vehicles from the RHE goods vehicle fleet.

So the pace of vehicle replacement in Pickfords slowed down considerably, for they had every intention of retaining a modern fleet at the end of the disposals period.

The next phase came about in August 1956 when the Transport (Disposal of Road Haulage Property) Act, 1956 came into effect. This was really an amendment to the 1953 Act, for it authorised the BTC to retain 9064 vehicles, of which 325 were abnormal indivisible load carriers, and a further 989 'special' vehicles.

Five new companies were set up under the Act: BRS (Parcels) Ltd., BRS (Meat Haulage) Ltd., BRS Ltd., BRS (Pickfords) Ltd., and BRS (Contracts) Ltd. From September 1956 these new companies had control of some 15,000 vehicles, with 1350 being allocated to Pickfords, 1000 to contracts and 500 to the meat haulage company.

At the Commercial Motor Show of that year an Austin vehicle was displayed bearing the new, more elaborate insignia of the new BRS, and this was soon to be seen on the doors of all the vehicles of the constituent companies. This Austin was a Meat Cartage vehicle and retained the fresh cream livery on the bodywork, contrasting with the standard Pickfords dark blue and black used on the chassis, cab and wings.

Both bonneted and forward control versions of the Austin were in service with meat haulage, many of them with insulated containers. Bedford S-type tractors and rigids were also in use, some of them with Leyland diesel engines. For long distance work there were a number of

Below: Not all loads have to be carried on a vehicle or trailer — this batching plant has been adapted so that part of its framework forms a trailer frame, to which a fixed axle and a turntable and drawbar enable it to be quickly and safely handled by this short wheelbase tractor unit of the Heavy Haulage department. This vehicle is one of the Atkinsons acquired as an alternative to the long-standing Scammells of the fleet, and is pictured heading south down the M1 motorway in 1970.

Right: The almost-completely exclusive Bedford hold on the Household Removals department was finally broken during the late 1950s when a number of Guy 4-ton 'Vixen' chassis were taken into the fleet. This was not the first time that Guys had been used, for many were absorbed into the New Furniture Carriage Service earlier in the decade and they had shown reliability in service. Compare this road-weary van, pictured towards the end of its days, with the pristine example on page 86.

Right: Traffic between Britain and Continental Europe during the 1960s, was handled by vehicles such as this articulated Bedford TK, seen here in the plain dark blue livery, with just a little French titling to underline the international connections. For very many years vehicles turned out at the Enfield bodyshops of Express Motor Bodyworks were taken the mile or so to Bullsmoor Lane to be photographed. On this occasion the vehicle is posed on the bridge over the New River, and Capel Manor is just visable in the distance.

Leylands with drawbar trailers, and later on these were augmented by a fleet of Guy articulated outfits, as the era of the vehicle and trailer configuration drew to a close.

Household Removals were running a large fleet of Guy 'Vixen' pantechnicons but a number of Ford 'Trader' Luton vans were added, as were a considerable number of A-type Bedfords, normal control Austins and a few Morris vans. Later on the Ford D-series appeared in the fleet, plus a number of Austin and Bedford tractor units.

Although the Scammell still formed the mainstay of the Heavy Haulage part of the business, there were changes taking place, with new marques appearing in varying roles. The Commer was taken into the fleet, these being the tractor version of the range for use with the lighter types of drop-frame trailers.

A number of Seddons with Leyland engines were acquired, plus some Atkinsons with Gardner engines, these handling work considered too heavy for the Commers. The new types of Scammell tractors soon appeared in the fleet, some with Albion engines, others with the standard Leyland 680. These included both articulated and ballasted versions.

The Tank Haulage fleet consisted mainly of AEC rigid eight-wheel chassis with either mild steel or stainless steel tanks according to the loads carried. Pickfords were large users of the AEC rigid eights, ranging from the early Mark IIs through the Mark III era, onto the Mark V and then into the tilt-cab G8RA version.

In a minor way other makes appeared, including Atkinson rigid-8s and tractors, the latter as replacements for the older Scammells, many of which had been acquired from other operators. There were also Leyland 'Beaver' tractors, plus some forward control Austins, Ford 'Trader', Bedford 'S' articulated tractors and later on those unusual bonneted Atkinsons in both four- and six-wheel form.

Of smaller dimensions, the Contract Hire fleet was expanded by considerable numbers of Austin, Bedford, Commer, Ford, Morris, Guy and even a few Karrier vans, but with their bespoke liveries they were not so readily recognisable as the familiar blue fleet.

The next major change came in January 1963 when the British Transport Commission was finally wound up, and control of the publicly-owned road transport companies passed to the new Transport Holding

Below: The tremendous increase in bulk traffic during the 1960s was met by the addition of several types of new articulated tankers designed to take advantage of the relaxed construction and use regulations of 1964 which gave rise to the introduction of 32-ton gross machines carried on five axles. Three-axle Atkinson tractors were obtained in both forward (see page 100) and normal-control layouts for movement of plastic moulding pellets and powders by means of twin tipping tanks mounted on framed trailers.

Right: Super Constructor M2211 entered service with Pickfords in March 1960 and, as a departure from normal practice, featured left-hand drive. It is seen here in that year heading up the 200-ton Crane girder trailer TM413 conveying a 150-ton Parsons stator to Rugeley power station. With the trailer alone weighing over 80 tons it is not surprising that assistance was required, although with three further examples bringing up the rear in all probability the function on this occasion was to provide extra braking capacity on a downward grade. Power for the Super Constructor was provided by the Leyland/Albion 15.2 litre 900 engine.

Right: Pickfords over the water — a scene in Liege, Belgium in 1965, as one of the old rubber-sprung Scammell tank trailers, bounces over a railway level crossing behind a Mercedes-Benz of Societe Belgo-Anglaise des Ferry-Boats SA. Early cross-channel journeys were often fraught with problems associated with non-compatible fifth-wheel positioning, brake couplings, light connections and spare wheels.

Company. Following this, BRS (Pickfords) Ltd. became just Pickfords Ltd., the title used previous to nationalisation in 1948.

1965 was quite an eventful year for the company, for it saw the takeover of Gavin Wilkie, the Scottish heavy haulier with 20 vehicles. Then in a few weeks came the news that negotiations had been concluded for the THC to acquire 75% of the capital of the Tayforth Group, a major transport group covering a wide variety of operations with 1500 vehicles. Much of this was absorbed into BRS but the bulk tanker part of the business was put under the control of Pickfords.

Next came the news that the 540-strong tanker fleet of Harold Wood & Sons had been acquired and was to be attached to Pickfords. This actually doubled the size of Pickfords tanker fleet overnight. Harold Wood & Sons was originally established in 1920, was taken over by Norcros in 1960, and had depots at Heckmondwike, Widnes, Basildon, Cardiff and Stockton. At that time Pickfords 425 tankers were based mainly at Stratford, Bootle and Manchester.

Within a short while another change came about, when BRS (Meat Haulage) Ltd. was merged with Union Cartage Co. Ltd. At that time the meat cartage fleet was around 200 vehicles operating from the bases in the Home Counties and at Southampton, Liverpool and Manchester.

In January 1969 the Transport Holding Company was wound up, and control placed in the hands of a National Freight Corporation. Pickfords was gradually reconstituted as separate companies according to their specialist function, so forming Removals, Heavy Haulage, Tankers, etc.

From January 1971 the companies became known as Pickfords Removals Ltd., Pickfords Tank Haulage Ltd., Pickfords Heavy Haulage Ltd., and Pickfords Management Services Ltd., with their headquarters being located at Finsbury Park, Holborn and Enfield. Pickfords (Contracts) Ltd., was transferred to BRS Ltd.

Later in the years, Pickfords International was formed by the amalgamation of Containerway Europe Ltd., Pickfords Shipping & Forwarding Co. Ltd., and Road-Air Cargo Express (International) Ltd. The new company was actually operational from March 1972 when the old Containerway Germany became Pickfords International GMBH, and Containerway Belgium renamed NV Pickfords International SA.

In 1972 the tank haulage operations of Pickfords, plus those of Harold Wood & Sons and Caledonian Bulk Liquids, both the subject of earlier takeovers, were merged to form Tankfreight Ltd.

During the 1970s the various parts of the fleet were replaced as necessary, and further changes took place. In Household Removals the

Right: Parking up for the night! Evidence of the roadside lanterns behind Scammell Constructor M4964 would suggest that this is the case. This September 1969 picture of a typical Scammell Constructor/Crane trailer combination assembled to convey the Crompton Parkinson transformer to its destination epitomises a time when the Watford product reigned supreme in both the fleet of Pickfords and other heavy haulage operators of the day.

Above: Pickfords maintained accurate records of their fleet, and in the case of the Heavy Haulage department, even went as far as issuing a book showing drawings of the tractors and trailers currently in use. This drawing of a Scammell 6x4 'Constructor' comes from a 1966 publication and shows the basic dimensions together with notes, including the fact that fully operational the vehicle weighed 46-tons unladen!

Right: Ready for the road — this works photo of Scammell Contractor M4847 when new illustrates the rugged yet classic line of the manufacturers then premier product. The ancestry of the four-door crew cab can be clearly be traced back to that of the Super Constructor model. The example illustrated was rated at 240 tons train weight but Pickfords were also to introduce into their fleet a considerable number of the smaller weight Contractor, these being rated by them as 100-tonners.

Bedford TK came to play a major role, both in its normal form as well as with specialist bodywork by Vanplan. The beefier KM also started to appear, plus a small number of the larger TM range.

Completely new to Pickfords was the Scania chassis, and a number of 80 models were brought into the fleet on removals work. Within a few years these were followed by a number of Mercedes Benz vans, again new to Removals although not quite the first in the fleet, for Pickfords did acquire their first way back in 1931.

The Heavy Haulage fleet was also seeing some new faces in the shape of Guy 'Big J', Volvo F88 and the MAN six wheel tractors with left-hand steering. A few Leyland 'Mastiff' tractors were also added for the lighter work, plus a number of Barreiros Dodge tractors. These latter machines were imported from Spain following the Chrysler takeover of the old Spanish truck builder, and appeared in the fleet at the same time as a batch of Chrysler 'Avenger' staff cars.

The 1970s heavies included Scammell 'Contractor', 'Handyman' and 'Crusader' models together with the lone 'Samson'. The Atkinsons embraced both normal- and forward-control tractors, including those with the Viewline cabs. In the Tank Haulage fleet Foden S80 tractors put in an appearance together with Seddon-Atkinson, ERF and Ford 'Transcontinental' models.

The later years of the decade were boom years for the NFC with increased profits being recorded in 1978 and 1979.

The recession of the early 1980s brought about a complete reversal of business, and there were reports of up to 1000 jobs being lost at NFC.

The downturn in the economy hit heavy haulage particularly hard, and it was decided to rename that section of the business, Pickfords Industrial Ltd., so as to more accurately reflect its on-going operations.

Following the Transport Act which effectively denationalised the NFC, there was a management buy-out, with the majority of the employees taking up shares in the new company.

As the economy gradually revived in the mid-1980s there followed a number of new developments. Pickfords Espana was established with headquarters in Madrid, Hoults Ltd. of Newcastle-upon-Tyne joined the company, but continued to operate separately. Pitt & Scott Ltd. was taken over and attached to Hoults, as was Hilton Removals, established in 1882 at

Below: The middle 1960s saw Pickfords establish a new contract service for Corn Products Ltd. with the use of three maximum capacity articulated bulk tank outfits operating at the 19-tons payload within the 32-ton gross limitation. One feature of the twin-tank design was that single tyres were used where possible, only the Atkinson tractor drive axle having twin tyres. The high load carrying capacity of the Michelin D20 tyres on the tractor and F20 type on the semi-trailer helped to keep weight down. In this photograph one of the outfits is seen on the M6 motorway heading for a delivery at Paisley.

Bottom right: Almost echoing the Scammell 100-tonner of some 40 years earlier, the ultimate Scammell operated by Pickfords was the 'Samson' 8x4 unit designed to operate at 75-tons gross weight. With a grp cab as used on the current 'Crusader' range from which it was derived, this one-off vehicle was exhibited at the 1970 Commercial Motor Show. It featured the General Motors V8 two-stroke diesel of 9.31 litres capacity which developed 290bhp, which seems very meagre by today's standards.

Right: Photographed on the M1 motorway in June 1970 when it was fresh out of the paintshops, this Guy 'Big J' articulated tanker shows the livery adopted by the Tank Haulage fleet at that time. The six compartment tank is a spirit type and a variation of the older elliptical section vessel favoured for its lower centre of gravity. The front mounted twin ladder arrangement is an improvement on older designs where the ladder was mounted at the side, and the filling manways along the top are surrounded by a raised section which prevents accidental spillages running down the tank sides.

Burgess Hill. John Julian of Cornwall was another old-established (1836) removal company to join in 1986, and in the same year Pickfords acquired its own Coat-of-Arms which can be displayed on the company vehicles.

In more recent years, with the restructuring of the parent company, vehicles with the Pickfords name displayed have centred on the removal side of the business. Ford 'Cargo', Volvo F7 and the Bedford TL models make up the bulk of the fleet, with a smattering of MAN and Iveco for special duties.

In 1988 agreement was reached with Allied Van Lines in the USA whereby Pickfords acquired control of the organisation. Following this takeover of the largest removal network in the United States, the new title of Allied Pickfords was adopted for the world-wide operations of the new combine. The orange livery of the American company was retained for the fleet engaged in corporate and international moving, with a complementary new blue livery incorporating the diagonal highway with its shield insignia for Pickfords Removals fleet operating within the UK.

In 1992, the company acquired the old established family business, Arthur Pierre, undisputed market leaders in Belgium and Luxembourg extending also into France, Netherlands and Spain. This major push into mainland Europe has provided a springboard to the new Eastern European market and Allied Pickfords' striking orange livery already brightens up a dull Moscow day.

With the approach of a new millenia, Pickfords continues to export its remarkable removal and relocation skills into new markets, capitalising on the increasing mobility of families within the new Single European Market. As both the CIS and Far East play an increasingly more important role in the global economy, Pickfords are at the forefront extending their unique global network to service both the business and diplomatic communities — a solid, comforting reminder of home in a new and often hostile environment.

Above: Following the demise of the company's own bodybuilding facilities, a variety of specialist commercial bodybuilders have been used to supply bodywork for the vehicle fleet. Pictured alongside the River Thames at low tide, close to the famous 'London Apprentice' public house at Isleworth, one of the Marsden-bodied Bedfords clearly shows the styling adopted for the current fleet of maximum capacity vans. This particular example is lettered for the Office & Commercial Removals section, being equipped with a generous crew cab to house the porters, and employs a modified style of Bedford KM double section bumper to protect the glass fibre front end.

Top right: Seen here in June 1981 making delivery of a Jones docks crane to Millbay docks, Plymouth is M9602, a V8 Detroit powered, sleeper-cabbed, Scammell Crusader 6x4 tractor unit. The crane had been conveyed on a tandem-axle King trailer.

Below: The changing face of removal vehicles in the 1970s, is shown by the adoption of chassis built in continental Europe, for service with the International Removals and Storage fleet. The 1617 model Mercedes Benz on the left has a capacity of some 2100 cubic feet and a bunk for the crew in the overcab body extension. That on the left is a model 808 Mercedes with a body of just half that of its larger companion.

Left: Quite uncharacteristic of Pickfords fleet were the MAN model 38.320 'Jumbo' 6x6 150-ton heavy haulage tractors taken into service during the 1970s. This was the period when the fleet was undergoing a change of livery, vehicles appearing in pale blue paintwork with an orange colour name logo of the name Pickfords, with Heavy Haulage Ltd. appearing in the tail of the 'S'.

Below: Pickfords believe that it is often better to train existing staff who already have removals experience, to drive a heavy vehicle rather than take on new personnel who lack expertise in packing and portering. During the 1970s this Bedford TK was employed as one of the company's HGV Driver Training vehicles.

Top right: During the early 1970s the new livery shown here was adopted for the fleet. The old dark blue main body colour was retained, but a more stylish script style of lettering used together with a wide waistband of varying colour to designate the particular service. This 1982 Luton-bodied TK Bedford had a bright red body panel indicating the Removals and Storage section of the undertaking.

Middle right: A new operation launched during the 1980s was Home Speed, Pickfords home delivery service, aimed at providing a dedicated delivery service for some of the larger retailers in the home furnishing market. A plain overall white livery was chosen for the new service, with the distinctive logo and lettering being carried out in red and blue. This turbocharged Bedford TL was just one of the large fleet of over 350 vehicles and trailers engaged in this service which was curtailed through the recession of the 1990s.

Bottom right: Complete with GB sticker and TIR plate, this Marsden-bodied Dodge is pictured in well-worn state at the end of its working life on long distance removals. The red waistband used with this livery, discontinued in 1992, carries the legend 'Local & International Removals & Homepack Storage'. The body has three pairs of full height doors on the nearside, providing easy access to the Homepack containers when loading, as well as unloading by forklift at the point of storage.

Left: In recent years the company has been keen to support vintage vehicles which have been presented in the company livery. Pictured alongside a 1985 Bedford in the Removals fleet is a restored example of the horsedrawn variety of a type that was used by many removal contractors in the days before mechanical traction, either steam or motor. The pair-horse van looks decidedly miniature alongside the modern Bedford, perhaps revealing that the modern household contains far more in the way of furniture and effects, than ever did the cottages of the last century.

As Pickfords removals became more involved in moving furniture and effects to a greater number of countries, and their sphere of influence spread to a more world-wide market, so a number of vehicles appeared in liveries reflecting the global image of the company and its operations. Some of the ordinary vans were repainted with the kangaroo logo *(above right)* to indicate the Australian connection, followed by purpose-built vans with tandem-axle close coupled drawbar trailers *(below)* turned out in the liveries of Pickfords Espana, and others embodying the German national flag, lettering and telephone number *(below left)*. The later adoption of the Allied Pickfords livery for overseas locations and the international removing business rendered these special liveries obsolete.

Left: Where large single consignments are moved, the use of close-coupled drawbar trailers carried on tandem running gear have come into use. This left-hand drive 1989 DAF 2500 rigid and trailer is being reversed into the storage facility at Enfield, which is one of the modern single-storey buildings designed to handle complete vehicles under cover. This van has the wide opening doors for loading the Homepack containers on its right-hand side for ease of access when working in continental Europe.

Below: Pictured at South Mimms services located at the junction of the M25 and A1M motorways, this 1986 Volvo F12 6x4 heavy haulage tractor and trailer awaits the arrival of a police escort. A number of Volvos are used in the Industrial fleet in both four- and six-wheel configurations, with some of the 6x4 tractors being equipped with ballast boxes and crew cabs. The vehicle is in the Pickfords Industrial blue livery with a white waistband and Haulage Division lettering as adopted in the 1980s.

Right: Taking a break at a motorway service area is one of the many Volvo FL617 vans used in the removal fleet. This vehicle is finished in the new livery with the roadway stripes, but is lettered as Pickfords 'The Business Movers', as opposed to 'The Careful Movers' which is used for the domestic removal fleet.

Below: Pictured in the 1980s style of designer script lettering, one of the many Volvo F6 vans is being loaded with the purpose built small containers which have proved invaluable for ease of handling and security for stored furniture and effects. With this type of container, the use of the Luton extension over the cab becomes redundant. Note the short vertical ladder at the nearside which leads to the sleeping compartment located behind the 'Executive Moving Service' banner.

Left: In the United States, Allied Van Lines was comparable to Pickfords Removals in Great Britain, it also being the largest in its field. By virtue of the greater expanse of the USA, the number of depots and vehicles was far in excess of that necessary to cover the British market for removals. This 1950s GMC articulated outfit shows the well-known orange and black livery, but lacks the Route 1 Shield logo which was adopted later.

Below: An example of the current fleet of vans used on removals work, is this maximum capacity on two axles Iveco-Ford 'Cargo' with crew cab. This vehicle is finished in the new livery adopted for the removal fleet early in 1992, soon after the setting up of Allied Pickfords. The rich dark blue ground colour is set off with an Anglicised version of the Allied Van Lines highway stripes and the Route 1 legend.

Right: As the company strives to provide even higher levels of service to its customers in the face of increasing competition, so the need for training becomes even more important. The Mobile Training Centre consists of a trailer fitted out as a classroom, complete with the latest teaching aids, and this is taken to any one of the 100 branches by the Leyland DAF 95 prime mover. This is in fact a full size removal van complete with a representative selection of typical household effects, together with the complete range of materials carried on every Household Removals van, including blankets, webbing, sack truck, piano wheels, etc.

Below: Typical of the modern Allied Pickfords fleet is this DAF 95 series articulated van with dropped frame and low profile tyres for a low floor height. This livery was adapted from the original layout used for the huge fleet of vehicles operating in the United States under the Allied banner. The disappearing black-topped roadway is emphasised by the white centre stripe and the US Highway Shield is used to denote No. 1 in the removals business.